# Fiscal Year 2015 National Environmental Information Exchange Network Grant Program Solicitation Notice

## Table of Contents

## Appendices

# Fiscal Year 2015 National Environmental Information Exchange Network Grant Program Solicitation Notice

## Overview Information

**Agency Name and Office:** U.S. Environmental Protection Agency (EPA), Office of Environmental Information (OEI)

**Funding Opportunity Title:** FY 2015 National Environmental Information Exchange Network Grant Program

**Announcement Type:** Availability of Funding Solicitation

**Notice Funding Opportunity Number**: EPA-OEI-15-01

**Catalog of Federal Domestic Assistance (CFDA) Number:** 66.608

**Dates:** November 24, 2014     - Deadline for submitting applications to EPA
July 31, 2015         - Expected Award of FY 2015 Exchange Network Grants

## I. Funding Opportunity Description

In FY 2015, the National Environmental Information Exchange Network (Exchange Network, Network or EN) Grant Program is focusing on Phase 2 of the EN and the incorporation of certain aspects of the E-Enterprise for the Environment (E-Enterprise or EE) initiative into the EN program. The general goals of the EE initiative align with the goals of the EN program, and, for this reason, the incorporation of certain EE initiatives into the EN program will further the goals of Phase 2.

The Exchange Network is a partnership that supports better decision-making through improved access to environmental information. EPA and agencies from states, tribes, and territories are collaboratively building the Network to improve the nation's ability to understand, protect, and preserve human health and the environment.

The aspects of the EE initiative that we are incorporating into the EN program will improve environmental outcomes and dramatically enhance service to the regulated community and the public by maximizing the use of advanced monitoring and information technologies, optimizing operations, and increasing transparency.

In addition to supporting similar goals, the EN and EE also affect similar stakeholders. EE began as joint U.S. Environmental Protection Agency (EPA)/state effort, and the EE leadership is reaching out to Indian Tribes to integrate them into this initiative.

While we believe the EE initiative activities that we are incorporating into the EN program are important, we maintain that it is also appropriate to continue to devote the significant majority of EN funds to continue to support the Phase 2 (and Phase 1) goals developed over the previous years (e.g., the implementation of new priority flows and the development of Web services/APIs and access tools and applications). For this reason, we are setting aside a portion of the EN funds for the new EE related activities. Eligible applicants (page 25) may apply for, and potentially be awarded two grants: one for traditional Phase 2 (or Phase 1) activities and one for the EE activities that are being incorporated into the EN program. We are phasing in the new EE related activities because we still have work to complete under Phase 2 of the EN program, and because we want to evaluate the effectiveness of the EE related activities prior to committing a larger portion of the limited resources available for the EN program. Applicants may apply for grants under one category or both, but they must submit separate applications for each grant for which they apply. The Agency will evaluate, score, and rank proposals under each category separately, and it will develop separate ranking lists for each category of EN grants. An award for an EE related grant will not exclude an applicant from receiving a traditional Phase 2 (or Phase 1) award for an EN grant and vice versa.

Exchange Network partners use Web services and standard data formats to electronically report, share, and integrate both regulatory and non-regulatory environmental information. Web services and machine-readable data formats allow for automated machine-to-machine communication over the Internet. EN partners can use those services to automate reporting requirements; integrate data sets for analysis, power mobile and desktop applications; support more efficient business processes; and be consistent with EPA's Open Data Policy[1]. More information about the Exchange Network is available at www.exchangenetwork.net.

The Exchange Network Grant Program provides funding to states, tribes, inter-tribal consortia and territories to develop and implement Web services, Web Application Programming Interfaces (APIs), and associated tools and applications that support efficient, open, and timely access to environmental data. Grantees will be required to register their work products in EPA's Reusable Component Services (RCS) database to promote discovery and reuse by other EN partners.

The focus of EE is on improving environmental outcomes. E-Enterprise is an initiative to fully integrate and streamline the way government protects the environment. Ideal E-Enterprise related projects for EN grants are those that improve efficiency, modernize programs, and reach across organizational boundaries.

## I-A. Background

***Exchange Network:*** EPA and its state, tribal, and territorial partners continue to invest collaboratively to expand the Exchange Network. Guided by the Exchange Network's Phase 2 implementation plan, approved by the Exchange Network Leadership Council in spring 2013, EPA and its partners will build upon the success of the Network's Phase 1 to enable timely, on-demand access to environmental data through innovative technologies, improved support systems, and expanded collaboration. In Phase 2, the Network community actively

---

[1] http://www.epa.gov/digitalstrategy/pdf/EPA_OpenDataPolicy_ImplementationPlan_2013Nov26.pdf

works to:

- build Web-based services and APIs that deliver environmental data in standard machine-readable formats;
- develop mobile, desktop, or Web applications that consume data via Web services and APIs and present information to users for analysis and access;
- expand the use of the Network for data reporting to EPA data systems;
- expand inter- and intra-partner data sharing including programs where EPA does not have a central data store (e.g. institutional controls for cleanup sites);
- expand the use of the Network for meeting goals related to transparency and open data; and
- develop new technologies that make data sharing easier and less costly.

To date, Exchange Network partners have almost exclusively used Exchange Network Node or Node Client software to submit or publish data via Web services[2]. Nodes and Node Clients will continue to be important tools for EN partners into the future, particularly for supporting secure reporting to EPA data systems. However, with Phase 2's emphasis on data access and availability, the Exchange Network Leadership Council (ENLC) and the Network Technology Board (NTB) are actively embracing additional approaches to Web service development that complement the traditional Node-based services.

RESTful Web services and APIs may offer partners a simpler and more flexible alternative for meeting certain business needs, such as lightweight data publishing and mobile application development. The NTB has developed guidance and standards for partners that wish to build RESTful Web services and APIs. Applicants should review that guidance for an explanation of REST and the options available for building EN-compliant REST services[3].

In their project descriptions, applicants should propose a design approach (with or without a Node) that best meets their business needs and is consistent with Exchange Network guidance and standards. Applicants should also make data available in eXtensible Markup Language (XML). As business needs dictate, applicants are also encouraged to offer data in additional machine-readable formats such as JSON and CSV.

**E-Enterprise:** E-Enterprise grew out of a recognition by environmental regulatory agencies that they needed to streamline the way they do business. As EPA began to develop its policy of converting paper reporting to E-Reporting, the Agency realized that the process has to include its co-implementers as well as a thorough update of both business processes and the use of technology, an effort that many of EPA's state partners have already begun. EPA, and states acting through the Environmental Council of States (ECOS), agreed that it made sense to pursue this process together. In September 2013, ECOS and EPA signed a charter to create the E-Enterprise Leadership Council (EELC). As EPA issues the 2015 Solicitation Notice, the E-Enterprise Leadership Council is working with the tribes to include them in the partnership.

With the limited funding available this year for the new EE related activities that are being

---

[2] http://www.exchangenetwork.net/exchange-network-products/
[3] The document is available at: http://www.exchangenetwork.net/rest-guidance/

incorporated into the EN program, EPA will focus on a few priorities (described in section I.E.2 on page 16), including business process analysis and reengineering and business architecture development. EPA will only accept E-Enterprise related project proposals from partnerships to maximize the value of this work.

The statutory authority for the Fiscal Year (FY) 2015 Exchange Network Grant Program will be the State and Tribal Assistance Grant (STAG) heading in EPA's Fiscal Year 2015 appropriation. The FY 2015 President's Budget requests $9,964,000 for the National Environmental Information Exchange Network activities. Funding of grant applications under this Solicitation Notice is subject to the availability of program funds in the FY 2015 annual appropriation for EPA. EPA is making $1.4 million of EN program funds available for projects implementing E-Enterprise activities that are being incorporated into the EN program.

## I-B. Grant Program Funding History and Results

FY 2015 is the fourteenth year EPA will be awarding Exchange Network grants. From FY 2002 through FY 2014, EPA provided approximately $190 million for state, tribal and territorial awards and associated program support through the grant program. As of May 2014, all 50 states, 94 tribes and 5 territories have received Exchange Network grants[4]. For information on the progress of the data exchanges, see http://www.exchangenetwork.net/. This year, for the first time, EPA is making grant funding available for E-Enterprise related projects.

## I-C. Assistance Activities

This Solicitation Notice requests that states, tribes, inter-tribal consortia, and territories develop and submit applications that support the Exchange Network or E-Enterprise priorities in Section I-E. For Exchange Network proposals, applications must commit to and clearly describe the development and implementation of EN tools and services reusable by other partners or the development and implementation of technologies and services directly related to Exchange Network activities. Examples of EN activities are in Section I-E and in Appendix A. Applicants may propose projects that include activities other than those listed as examples, provided they are consistent with EN priorities and conform to Exchange Network technologies, services and specifications. For E-Enterprise related EN proposals, applications must explain how the project can be replicated by other states and tribes and how the grant funded work will benefit the Exchange Network and be consistent with E-Enterprise principles. Building on previous EN grant priorities that were focused on data exchange, the EE-related work must benefit the overall E-Enterprise initiative, including harmonized rulemaking, streamlined business processes, and advanced monitoring.

EPA will determine the eligibility of each applicant (see Section III-A). EPA will then evaluate applications from eligible applicants based on the evaluation criteria in Section V-

---

4 For descriptions of previously awarded Exchange Network Grants, please see:
http://www.epa.gov/exchangenetwork/grants/index.html

A. Applicants are responsible for reading and complying with the instructions and criteria found in this Notice.

## I-D. Environmental Results Supported by Assistance Activities

EPA's mission is to protect human health and the environment. Timely access to information supports strong environmental decision-making and improves the ability of EPA, with its state and tribal partners, to carry out that mission. The Exchange Network helps states, territories, tribes, and EPA share environmental information more efficiently and effectively over the Internet. Phase 2 of the Exchange Network will make data critical for decisions more readily available. Efficient sharing of and increased access to high-quality data among EN partners strengthens their ability to make sound environmental decisions including improved priority setting and resource targeting. E-Enterprise will support EPA's mission by streamlining and reducing the burden of business operations, fully integrating Exchange Network technology and services into business operations, and increasing the use of advanced monitoring technologies to improve environmental outcomes and increase building on the achievements of the Exchange Network. E-Enterprise is an initiative to improve environmental outcomes and increase transparency.

Applications under this Solicitation must clearly demonstrate support of the EPA 2014-2018 Strategic Plan, Cross-Agency Strategies, Objective of "Launching a New Era of State, Tribal, Local, and International Partnerships"[5]. It is EPA policy to directly link work supported by assistance agreements to the Agency's mission and Strategic Plan. Grant applications, assistance agreements, and work plans must all have outcomes that lead to or are instrumental in achieving environmental results supporting the Agency's mission and Strategic Plan goals.

Applications for E-Enterprise-related EN projects under this Solicitation should also support the EPA September 30, 2015 Agency Priority Goal to "Improve environmental outcomes and enhance service to the regulated community and the public." The goal states, "By September 30, 2015 reduce reporting burdens to EPA by one million hours through streamlined regulations, provide real-time environmental data to at least two communities, and establish a new portal to service the regulated community and public[6]. Consistent with EPA's goal, states, tribes, and territories should address similar goals to reduce reporting burdens to their own agencies, support cross-agency sharing of real-time environmental data, and establishing interoperable state and EPA portals.

---

[5] EPA's 2014-2018 Strategic Plan can be found at: http://www2.epa.gov/planandbudget/fy-2014-2018-strategic-plan
[6] EPA's 2014-2015 Agency Priority Goal can be found at http://www.performance.gov/node/360?view=public#apg

## Goals, Outputs, Outcomes and Environmental Results

EPA recognizes that Exchange Network and E-Enterprise-related EN projects do not *directly* produce environmental results and will therefore evaluate applications based on the major technical and non-technical outputs and outcomes of the proposed work. **Each proposed goal should have at least one outcome the applicant expects will lead to or be instrumental in achieving an environmental result.**

---

*Examples of Project Outputs:*
- development of schema
- development of Web services and application programming interfaces (APIs) that enable data publishing
- establishment of new interagency processes, advanced monitoring systems, portals, or shared services
- issuance of Requests for Proposals (RFPs)

*Examples of Project Outcomes:*
- improving the timeliness and accuracy of environmental data
- reducing burden and costs associated with data management and reporting
- increasing access to environmental data from program systems or real-time environmental data from advanced monitoring systems
- supporting better decision-making by building data access for environmental professionals and the public
- facilitating place-based decision-making through the inclusion of quality locational data which transcend jurisdictional boundaries
- streamlining and harmonizing source environmental regulations and policies to avoid inconsistent, redundant, or cumulative burden
- achieving operational efficiencies and reducing burden for regulated entities and citizens through new interagency processes or shared services

---

Figure 1-1 below presents an example workplan for an **Exchange Network** project showing the relationship of goals, outcomes and outputs leading to environmental results.

**Figure 1-1: Exchange Network Project example**

| Goal 1 – Electronic Notice of Intent (eNOI) and eForms | Goal 1 Outcome(s) |
|---|---|
| | 1. Increased availability of timely, high quality data to other Exchange Network Partners will improve environmental decision–making.<br><br>2. Increases efficiency needed to review and process notice of intent applications, allowing program implementation resources to be spent on other environmental needs. |
| **Output** | **Scheduled Date** |
| 1.1 Design and develop Microsoft.Net Web forms/pages for each NOI. | January 2016 |
| 1.2 Design and develop eForms to TEMPO automated data migrations. | February 2016 |
| 1.3 TEMPO administrative review and technical review automation and quality verification routines. | March 2016 |
| 1.4 Create and Implement GIS active data layers. | December 2016 |
| 1.5 Create and implement ICIS-NPDES XML data flows, flow data using State Node to Exchange Network Node. | December 2016 |

- Each goal should result in a major deliverable, such as a sustained dataflow.
- Applications should list and schedule major outputs that lead to achieving a goal.
- Each goal should have at least one outcome that leads to environmental results.

Figure 1-2 below presents an example workplan for an **E-Enterprise-related EN** project showing the relationship of goals, outcomes and outputs leading to results that streamline a source environmental policy or the services for implementing that policy.

**Figure 1-2: E-Enterprise Related EN Project example**

| Goal 1 – Federated Identity for Regulatory Reports in State X and Tribe Y | Goal 1 Outcome(s) |
|---|---|
| | 1. Integrate with a federated bridging solution that will allow a business to reuse a single set of credentials (e.g. user ID and password) for environmental sector services across multiple levels of government.<br><br>2. Integrate the bridging solution in zz reports for affected regulated entities in State X and Tribe Y. It is estimated that 25,000 regulated entities submitting this report must also directly report to other EPA regulatory reporting systems. This will reduce burden for identification and authentication across federal and state governments by 1,250 hours annually. |
| **Output** | **Scheduled Date** |
| 1.1 Analysis and redesign of zz reporting system to accept protocols and standards for TFS. | January 2016 |
| 1.2 Communications plan for existing and new users describing new process for identity management. | March 2016 |
| 1.3 User acceptance testing in test environment. | June 2016 |
| 1.4 Transition of user accounts and move new identity system to production. | August 2016 |
| 1.5 Use-case documentation and lessons learned for distribution to other E-Enterprise stakeholders. | October 2016 |

- Each goal should result in a major deliverable, such as a streamlined service or new shared service.
- Applications should list and schedule major outputs that lead to achieving a goal.
- Each goal should have at least one outcome that leads to results that streamline a source environmental policy or the services for implementing that policy.

## I-E. Program Priorities

EPA expects Exchange Network assistance agreement supported projects will improve the exchange of and access to high-quality environmental data from public and private sector sources.

## I-E.1. Exchange Network Priorities

In FY 2015, the Exchange Network community will be fully engaged in Phase 2 development efforts. For prospective applicants not familiar with the current focus of the Exchange Network, Phase 2 emphasizes making data available through Web services and application programming interfaces (APIs), inter-partner data sharing and reporting to new national priority systems. This is in contrast to the first phase of the Network, which focused more on grantees reporting regulatory data to EPA as mentioned in the Phase 2 Implementation Plan[7].

EPA will place a high priority on activities that advance Phase 2 goals. These include: development of Web services and APIs that deliver automated access to environmental data; reusable tools and applications that support data access and analysis and are built to consume Web services and APIs; new regulatory reporting data flows; use of Virtual Node services; and use of Cross Media Electronic Reporting Regulation (CROMERR) compliant shared services. EPA recognizes that partners continue to implement automated reporting to the 10 EPA National Priority data systems that were the focus of Phase 1. EPA will support states, federally recognized tribes and territories in completing these priority flows through Exchange Network grant funding.

EPA is categorizing Exchange Network grant priorities into two tiers. In general, Tier 1 focuses on Phase 2 activities (development of Web services/APIs and access tools and applications, implementation of new priority flows, integration of virtual node services into a partner's information technology infrastructure, implementation of new national data exchanges). Tier 2 focuses on Phase 1 priorities including the implementation of the original 10 priority data exchanges and the reminder of Exchange Network related activities.

As described in Section V-A (evaluation criteria), applications that include at least one Tier 1 goal are eligible to receive 30 points. Applications that include at least one Tier 2 goal but no Tier 1 goal are eligible to receive 20 points.

No Exchange Network grant funds will be available to state, federally recognized tribes, intertribal consortia and territorial partners for node development projects. EPA is making available, and encourages all applicants to use, the Agency's new virtual node. Furthermore, operations and maintenance of flows is not an eligible activity for funding.

---

7 Available online at:
http://www.exchangenetwork.net/wp-content/uploads/2011/07/Phase_2_Implementation_Plan.pdf

## Tier 1 Exchange Network Activities:

➢ **Development of Web Services/APIs and Tools that Promote Data Access and Support Better Environmental and Public Health Decisions.** Applications will include projects that improve access to environmental information for environmental program staff, managers, the public and other stakeholders. Projects will include goals that lead to the creation of Web services and APIs that make data available in XML and other standard machine-readable formats (e.g. JSON, CSV). Applicants should consider opportunities to share data across programs within their organization; across agencies within a state or tribe; or with EPA. Applicants should also consider opportunities to build Web services and tools that support EPA's open data and transparency goals and serve interested non-governmental organizations, research institutions, and the public.

Example activities include:
- Creating Web services and APIs that make data available in XML and other machine-readable formats.
- Creating Web services and APIs that support cross-program data integration and support more efficient environmental business processes such as permit writing or compliance inspections or cross-jurisdictional data comparisons analyses or integration.
- Creating tools that consume Web services and APIs to support access and analysis of environmental information. Examples of such tools include:
  - Desktop, laptop, mobile, and Web applications that allow users to display, analyze, or collect environmental information.
  - Web sites that allow users to access environmental data sets that are available through Exchange Network Web services or APIs.
  - Dashboards for program managers, EPA and other Agency executives.

Example datasets may include institutional controls at contamination sites, data on cleanup sites, data sets of national significance to tribes (such as open dumps), Underground Storage Tank data, and data that support environmental management of multi-state or regional airsheds, watersheds, and water bodies of priority concern (such as the Great Lakes or Chesapeake Bay). See appendix A for more detail on specific project opportunities.

Grantees must use either existing EN-based services, APIs, and schemas or new EN-based services, APIs, and schemas that conform to Exchange Network standards and design rules. This includes REST-based APIs that conform to the Network's REST guidance and standards. Information on the Network's technical standards and design guidance are available in the Knowledge Base of the Exchange Network website (http://www.exchangenetwork.net/knowledge-base). Grantees must register grant-funded data flows and Web services in the Exchange Network Discovery Service (ENDS). Grantees must register grant-funded tools, applications, schemas, and other reusable resources in the EPA Reusable Components Service (RCS).

Specific Tier 1 activities include:

➤ **New EPA Reporting Data Flows.** Applications will include goals to implement data flows that enable Exchange Network reporting to and from EPA data systems. Applicants must commit to register these data flows in ENDS. The new flows include:
  - Integrated Compliance Information System – Air (ICIS-Air), which will replace the Air Facility System or AFS;
  - Safe Drinking Water Information System (SWDIS) Prime;
  - Electronic Notice of Intent (eNOI) flow to Integrated Compliance Information System – National Pollutant Discharge Elimination System (ICIS-NPDES);
  - eManifest
  - Radon and
  - Assessment TMDL Tracking & ImplementatioN System (ATTAINS)

➤ **Virtual Node Implementation Support for States, Tribes, and Territories.** Applicants should commit to the transition from locally installed nodes to the EPA-hosted Virtual Node, creation of data publishing services and new data flows on the Virtual Node and support Virtual Node-related security analyses and plans. Applicants must commit to register all virtual nodes in ENDS. Appendix B provides a detailed description of the Virtual Node and suggested implementation activities.

➤ **Shared CROMERR Services and Components.** Applicants will commit to the design of systems to use one or more EPA Web services that provide CROMERR compliant functionality, such as electronic signature, to reduce or eliminate redundant development by partners and streamline Technical Review Committee (TRC) application reviews. Applicants must commit to register these tools in RCS. Appendix C provides a detailed description of the EPA CROMERR services.

Examples of specific potential projects related to these broad topics include:

➤ **ICIS-Air Collaborative Opportunity:** A partnership application that includes joint state, local government or a regional or national Clean Air Act association to create a tool that facilitates the exchange of CAA stationary source compliance and enforcement data between and among state agencies, air pollution control districts or local agencies and EPA. The focus of this opportunity is to enable states and locals to develop and implement a common tool to easily exchange data using the EN with the modernized Air Facility System (AFS), ICIS-Air. EPA plans to deploy ICIS-Air in 2015. **Applications should clearly identify all partners and their roles and responsibilities. The lead applicant must be an eligible entity (Section III-C). Projects eligible for the partnership level funding must include two or more states. Partnerships eligible for this opportunity may have state or local agencies from two or more states or by having a Clean Air Act association with members that come from two or more states in the partnership.**

➤ **eReporting Collaborative Opportunity**: A partnership proposal that builds an eReporting system integrating one or more EPA Web services that provide CROMERR compliant functionality such as electronic signature. In order for this proposal to be eligible for funding, applicants must commit to flowing the reported data to EPA using the Exchange Network, which will provide a complete end-to-end electronic reporting solution for environmental data. An example of an e-reporting grant proposal would be Clean Air Act Title V reporting (such as annual compliance certifications).

➢ **Continuous Water Quality Monitoring Collaborative Opportunity:** A partnership to develop an exchange of water quality sensor data. Continuous water quality monitoring (monitoring performed with a sensor that measures a particular parameter or suite of parameters automatically at set intervals) is becoming more common. The EPA Office of Water (OW) is exploring options for enabling the exchange of this type of data. Several partners have been sharing summaries of this type of data using the Water Quality Exchange (WQX). WQX has worked well for sampling data, but the data model for sensor data is inherently different. It uses less metadata for more results. Because of this, approaches for sharing sensor data may also be different. This project would take advantage of current thinking on the publishing approaches defined under Phase 2 of the Exchange Network, as well as make use of the Exchange Network REST specification. EPA is evaluating approaches that would allow state, tribal and territorial partners to share sensor by using a publishing service from their node or via a cloud node. As a Phase 2 project, partners should consider approaches that would make water quality sensor data available via a publishing service that would allow for data to be cataloged and searched from a central portal. Project work plans should include a commitment to evaluate schemas developed for sharing this type of data, such as the recently approved Open Geospatial Consortium WaterML 2.0 standard[8] and the Sensor Observation Service[9]. The partnership would also work with EPA on defining approaches for integrating this information with sampling data made available from WQX, as well as providing public access to this combined set of information. Through this project, EPA is seeking to more fully represent the complete set of water quality data that is being collected by continuing to support WQX for water quality sampling data while identifying new approaches for sharing sensor data.


### Tier 2 Exchange Network Activities:

➢ **Phase 1 EPA Reporting Flows.** Additional funding for completing 10 priority flows as listed in Appendix K (Register in ENDS)
  - 1) **Implementation by an Exchange Network partner** (or partners) of any of the 10 flows for which an applicant has not received funding; or ,2) Addition of entirely new modules to existing dataflows. For example, adding an entire class of UIC reporting, adding a new RCRAInfo module, or adding a new data family under ICIS-NPDES.

➢ **Cross-Media Electronic Reporting Regulation (CROMERR)**. Development and deployment of CROMERR upgrades to an existing electronic reporting system, described

---

[8] http://www.opengeospatial.org/standards/waterml
[9] http://www.opengeospatial.org/standards/sos

in a CROMERR application previously approved by EPA, to bring it into compliance with the regulatory standards. Applicants must commit to registering these resources in RCS.

- **Collaborative Opportunity**. Partnership to develop multi-program CROMERR application for states that currently do not have an enterprise-wide approach or to adapt CROMERR solutions already approved by EPA that other states have implemented. (An application that additionally commits to using the new EPA components and services that will provide CROMERR-compliant functionality will be scored as a Tier 1 proposal.)

➤ **Collaborative Tribal Opportunity.** Tribal governments and inter-tribal consortia are eligible to apply for Exchange Network grants to build tribal capacity that will enhance environmental programs on tribal lands and a tribe's ability to share environmental data electronically with EN partners. Collaborative tribal capacity building proposals must include multiple tribes and identify tribes with existing capacity that can serve as mentors. Collaborative tribal capacity proposals must identify specific outputs that result in the increased ability to share environmental information electronically with EPA or other EN partners (for example, developing a backend database for a priority data system).

➤ **Updating large national data sets.** Schema development effort that will enable states to flow data through the Exchange Network to update large national datasets that fall under Appendix E of OMB Circular A-16: "Coordination of Geographic Information and Related Spatial Data Activities." These datasets can include the National Hydrography Dataset (NHD), National Watershed Boundary dataset, National Wetland Inventory Dataset, National Elevation Dataset, Geographic Names Dataset and others listed in A-16.

In addition to the priority activities above, EPA programs have identified other activities listed in Appendix A. The tier for these other activities are in bolded, italicized text in Appendix A. For each data system in this appendix, the tier is identified either in a note directly following the list of activities for that system (if the activities are all in the same tier) or in parentheses after each activity if the activities within a system are in different tiers.

## I.E.2. E-Enterprise Priorities That are Being Incorporated into the EN Program

Consistent with the Exchange Network grant priorities, EPA is creating two tiers of EE related grant priorities in the EN program. Tier 1 focuses on activities that will lay the groundwork for a successful intergovernmental partnership to streamline and modernize the "enterprise" of environmental protection. Tier 2 focuses on immediate progress toward joint EPA, State, Tribal, and Territorial enterprise-wide performance goals for one million hours of regulatory burden reduction. In both tiers, EPA will only accept project proposals from partnerships, and the project outcomes must be transferrable to other partners.

As described in Section V-A (evaluation criteria), applications that include at least one Tier 1 goal are eligible to receive 30 points. Applications that include at least one Tier 2 goal, but no Tier 1 goal, are eligible to receive 20 points.

## Tier 1 E-Enterprise Related EN Activities:

> **Joint Enterprise Architecture (EA) Analyses.** The EPA has acquired federal contract support for an E-Enterprise EA analysis. A copy of the task order is available on www.epa.gov/exchangenetwork/grants . Although the contract task order is structured to be collaborative, the scope and available funding will have limited capacity to perform detailed analyses of internal state, tribal, and territorial programs. To support active contribution of intergovernmental analyses, the E-Enterprise and Exchange Network Leadership Councils have chartered the Enterprise Architecture Integrated Project Team (IPT). Applications cannot be limited to participation in joint IPT meetings. Projects must include significant analysis of business processes and systems within and across state/tribal and EPA governments. The projects must lead to qualifying outputs as described in Section V-A.2, and those outputs must adhere to guidelines and approaches established as part of this joint EA IPT.

In order to understand, protect, and preserve human health and the environment, the partner governments in the national enterprise of environmental protection must not only share data in a standardized way, but understand the context of the data and the interrelationships of the source programs, processes, and services that drive the information exchange. Enterprise architecture is a disciplined framework for analyzing these interrelationships and identifying more effective and efficient ways of coordinating among environmental regulators.

Example activities include:
- Strategic and Business Architecture: In support of Task 1 on the EPA contract, use reference models and other tools to conceptually organize and analyze strategic performance goals, mission functions, and business processes. This will help to identify the breadth of services offered across environmental agencies and establish a baseline for analyses of performance improvements and shared services.
- Functional Integration: In support of Task 3, identify groups of services within the environmental sector that support similar functional requirements across multiple programmatic and organizational silos. This would include intergovernmental services that share common customers and interact with those customers through similar mechanisms. For example, a qualifying application could propose cross-governmental analysis to identify shared services for reporting, permitting, financial assurance, labeling, registration, or signatures. This could also include cross-governmental policy harmonization or process improvement to address overlapping or inconsistent policies and procedures that inhibit the ability to offer shared or streamlined services.
- IT Resource Optimization: In support of Task 4, conduct inventories of existing IT systems that support transactions between environmental regulators and regulated entities and other citizens. This includes the underlying data, applications, and infrastructure in state and tribal governments. Identify gaps in technology services, including opportunities to convert remaining paper-based processes to technology services. Identify inefficiencies and

17

redundancies in existing IT systems and offer recommendations for new shared IT data, applications, and infrastructure, including cloud-based services, platforms or infrastructure.

- Support for Policy Mandates: In order to coordinate distributed systems and shared services, there need to be standardized methods for analyzing and documenting individual IT systems and broader IT portfolios. In establishing common methods and standards across governments, it is important to identify any applicable policy drivers. At the federal level, EA is addressed in a variety of policies, and the documentation of IT architectures plays an important role in budgeting for IT capital investments. Task 8 of the EPA EA contract includes the development of standardized tools and formats for EA documentation. Example grant projects could include an analysis of corresponding state and tribal level policy mandates and the development of EA tools and documentation formats that comply with those policy mandates.

- **Participation in Pilot Projects.** In addition to the broad and comprehensive Enterprise Architecture analysis, the EPA will be focusing on immediate opportunities for shared services that can both reduce burden and optimize IT resources. As was the case with the overall EA project, these efforts are intended to be collaborative and will require state, tribal, and territorial participation on IPTs. Applications cannot be limited to participation in joint IPT meetings. Projects must include significant development and integration of services within and across state/tribal and EPA governments. The projects must lead to qualifying outputs as described in Section V-A.2, and those outputs must adhere to guidelines and approaches established as part of joint IPTs.

The EN has traditionally been focused on data exchange. The systems that collect or publish the data, however, can involve redundant processes and supporting technologies. E-Enterprise principles support the natural next step in the evolution of the EN program to improve decision-making and environmental outcomes through a more comprehensive view of interrelated data and services.

Example activities include:
- Federated Identity: The EPA is seeking opportunities to allow regulated entities to use a common set of credentials (e.g. login and password) across multiple environmental agencies and levels of government. To accomplish this in the most efficient manner possible, the EPA is researching the development of a single bridging solution. This federated bridge would accommodate a single identity for state/tribal-specific users and systems, CDX reporters, and users who would like to access My.USA.gov and other federal agency services that adhere to the Federal Identity Credential and Access Management (FICAM) trust framework solutions.
- Portals: The EPA is initiating a scoping project for the development of portals for consolidating and streamlining services and information for regulated entities and the public.
- Advanced Monitoring: The EPA has identified pilot initiatives for advanced monitoring, including the Village Green program. State, tribal, and territorial

participation is needed to support the implementation of these programs in at least two communities in fiscal year 2015.

- BPM Suites and Model-Driven Architecture: The EPA is implementing a pilot project for developing and coordinating environmental IT services from platform-independent models rather than hard-coded software. Grant funds can be applied to develop shared services for states and tribes using the same model-driven software suite.
- Mobile Solutions: The EPA is scoping the development of mobile platforms or device-agnostic services that can be accessed from multiple mobile devices. Specifically, the EPA is scoping the development of a National Inspection Evidence System, a tablet-based compliance inspection tool. Grant funds can support intergovernmental IPTs for scoping state inspection tools or other mobile solutions that support transactions with regulated entities.

➢ **Support for EELC Projects.** On January 21, 2014, the EELC adopted a Conceptual Blueprint. Operating Principle #3 in the Blueprint is to "Modernize and Improve Environmental Regulations and Programs, and their Implementation." In support of this effort to improve efficiency and performance, the Blueprint also includes Principle #4 for "Joint Governance Prioritizing Activities." Specifically, the Blueprint states "Within the context of an overall E-Enterprise business case analysis, this principle anticipates the use of a return-on-investment (ROI) to assist the EELC in implementation decisions. The business case information and methods will also enable the measurement of progress and inform ongoing management of the initiative."

The EELC began work on a prioritized list of action items from the Blueprint, including an action item to identify a list of potential E-Enterprise modernization and streamlining projects. On March 21, 2014, the EELC directed a Coordinating Team to manage the process of soliciting project proposals, including performing an initial screening of the projects and presenting them to the Leadership Council for further consideration. On March 31, 2014, the EELC Co-Chairs kicked off a solicitation to collect project modernization proposals from States, EPA Headquarters, EPA Regions and others. During an E-Enterprise Leadership Council Meeting on May 22-23, 2014, the Council reviewed and evaluated 84 submitted proposals. The following five proposals were selected for further scoping and analysis:

- Promote availability and use of water data for water resource protection.
- Explore integrating and streamlining air emissions reporting
- Investigate business process improvements and smart mobile technology tools to support state and EPA inspectors.
- Develop a "smart pesticide label" to improve the accuracy and effectiveness of the label in promoting safe pesticide use.
- Pilot a compliance assistance and community service tool for local governments

The EPA has acquired federal contract support for the scoping of proposals that have been prioritized by the E-Enterprise Leadership Council (EELC). To support active contribution of intergovernmental partners, the E-Enterprise and Exchange Network

Leadership Councils are forming Integrated Project Teams (IPTs) with co-chairs from EPA and state/tribal representatives.

Grant applications may be submitted to support EELC priority projects. To ensure the widest benefit and adoption rate among qualified grant recipients, applications will not be limited to the original participants in the IPTs. Award of the grants will be contingent on approval of the project scoping analyses by the EELC, which will depend on a sound business case and a positive return on investment. The EELC approval must precede the convening of the grant proposal review panels. There are no guarantees that any or all of the scoping efforts will be completed soon enough to achieve EELC approval prior to the grant reviews.

Regardless of whether the EELC approved the scoping analysis, there are no guarantees that the projects will receive grant funding. The applications will be considered together with other Tier 1 and Tier 2 applications, and all projects will undergo the same review and selection process described in Section V-B. They will be subject to the same evaluation criteria described in Section V-A.2. In order to achieve Tier 1 status, the proposals must substantively align with the projects described in the original scoping proposals.

➤ **Modernizing the Legal Framework.** Consistent with federal Executive Orders 12866, 13563 and 13610, the EPA is planning new regulations and retrospectively reviewing existing regulations to identity opportunities for regulatory burden reduction. Grant funds can support corresponding projects that address the roles of delegated partners at the state, tribal, and territorial level of government.

Example activities include:
- Regulatory Reviews: Establishing policies and processes for tracking the relationships between federal and state regulations and identifying inefficiencies, redundancies, and cumulative burden in how EPA and the state collaborate to implement a policy.
- E-Regulations: Establishing IT tools to support the tracking and analysis of regulations. For example, information systems are used by the Federal Office of Management and Budget, EPA, and various state and tribal programs to track the progress of active rulemakings. Through the appropriate use of metadata and application programming interfaces, these information systems could be useful in identifying the impact of new rulemakings on existing services, and evaluating whether the proposed rules could be harmonized with existing rules to minimize inefficiencies, redundancies, and cumulative burden. Similarly, information technologies could be helpful in accessing and analyzing existing codified regulations. Existing regulations could be analyzed for opportunities to harmonize rules or support enterprise architecture analyses for new paper-to-electronic conversions or new or improved shared services.

- Performance Projections: Performing analyses of compliance burden, including paperwork burden, and establishing projections of regulatory burden reduction from key regulatory reforms.

## Tier 2 E-Enterprise Related EN Activities:

➢ **Expand the Adoption of Existing Shared Services.** Projects will support the expanded use of shared services that streamline the delivery of environmental services to regulated entities. This is intended to focus on the "backend" services for policy implementation, rather than the existing efforts of the EN for networking and information exchange. This can also include non-IT efforts to streamline the delivery of services, such as improvements to intergovernmental policies and processes. All applications for projects in this category must include activities for performance analysis in the scope of their projects. The goal is to not only to adopt shared processes and services, but to measure burden and costs avoided through reuse.

Example activities include:
- Non-IT Process Improvements: This can include any efforts to streamline the delivery of services, such as intergovernmental policies and processes. Under the EN program, the focus has been on "how" to exchange data through improved standards and technologies. Non-IT process improvements can support environmental outcomes by evaluating "what" data should be exchanged or reused, and "when" and "why" services and information exchanges are performed in the first place.
- Reusing Data: This can include the integration of datasets made available from the EPA System of Registries and data published through the EN. The data would need to be integrated into the software services in a way that eliminates the redundant collection of similar data and achieves measurable burden reduction for regulated entities.
- Reusing IT Services and Infrastructure: This can include the intergovernmental sharing of services and supporting infrastructure. Grant funds can go toward the investment in the changes necessary to support the sharing of an existing service, such as moving the service to a third party cloud or establishing interfaces that can remotely call for the services (e.g. a private cloud).

➢ **Develop New Shared Services.** Additional projects for new shared services will only be selected if they are "shovel ready" projects that streamline the delivery of environmental services to regulated entities. These can include services that were not already identified for pilots or scoping activities by the EPA or EELC. The services must support the principles of E-Enterprise and forward the performance goals for regulatory burden reduction and new advanced monitoring approaches. The projects must demonstrate that an alternatives analysis was performed, including market research of existing government-off-the-shelf or commercial-off-the-shelf solutions. The projects must also demonstrate that the business needs and solution architecture have been established. All applications for projects in this category must include activities for performance analysis in the scope of their projects.

Example activities include:

- State/Tribal Level Solutions: This can include services that can be adopted by two or more partner governments at the state, tribal, or territorial levels.
- Integration at Multiple Levels of Government: This can include industry-to-state-to-EPA solutions similar to the model for federal and state taxes. For example, this could include the development of a service that reuses information submitted at the federal level, and only requires regulated entities to add the minimum information required to account for differences in state requirements.

## I-F. Partnership Agreements

*Project narratives and budgets should explain specifically why the proposed project requires additional resources available through a partnership assistance agreement. Reasons for additional funding may include project complexity or activities in support of partner collaboration.* Partnership applications may fall into Tier 1 or Tier 2; EPA will determine the appropriate tier based on the specific project proposals and the Program Priorities described in Section I-E. See Section III-C, "Eligibility Criteria for Partnership Applications," before making any financial commitments to project partners or listing these partners in an application.

## II. Award Information

The Catalog of Federal Domestic Assistance number for the Exchange Network Grant Program is 66.608 (http://www.cfda.gov).

## II-A. General Information

**Exchange Network.** In FY 2015, EPA expects to award about $10,000,000 for 40 to 50 assistance agreements of up to $500,000 each. The exact number of grants will depend on the final amount of EPA's appropriation for the grant program, the number of applications submitted to EPA by the application deadline, the amounts of proposed budgets, and the outcome of application reviews.

Most awards will be in the $50,000 to $300,000 range. **Awards to a single applicant cannot exceed $300,000. EPA may make a limited number of awards to collaborative, partnership assistance agreements. Budgets for these projects cannot exceed $500,000.** EPA remains committed to, at a minimum, awarding tribal assistance agreements equal to approximately 10 percent of the appropriated funds. The amount awarded to tribes may be greater than this minimum level, depending on the merit of tribal applications and on the competitive review of all applications. The standard period of performance for each project is three years. EPA expects to announce the FY 2015 Exchange Network Grant program awards in April 2015 and award the grants by July 31, 2015.

**EN Projects related to E-Enterprise.** In FY 2015, EPA expects to award about $1.4 million for three to four assistance agreements up to $500,000 each. For E-Enterprise assistance agreements, EPA is only accepting partnership applications.

For both Exchange Network and E-Enterprise assistance agreements, EPA reserves the right to partially fund applications by funding only proposed goals that the Agency believes to be eligible and appropriate Exchange Network/ E-Enterprise projects. If EPA decides to partially fund a project, it will do so in a manner that does not prejudice any applicants or affect the basis upon which EPA evaluated and selected the application or portion thereof for award, and therefore maintains the integrity of the competition and selection process.

**Additional Awards** EPA reserves the right to make additional awards under this announcement, consistent with Agency policy, if additional funding becomes available after the original selections. EPA will make any additional selections for awards no later than six months from the date of the original selections.

## II-B.  Types of Assistance

EPA may award assistance agreements funded through the Exchange Network Grant Program as grants or cooperative agreements, in-kind services or performance partnership grants. EPA will consider an applicant's preferences when the Agency decides what type of assistance to award.

EPA uses assistance agreement vehicles to transfer funding and services to a recipient to accomplish a public purpose. Unlike contracts, grants are structured and managed to ensure the project benefits the recipient toward the identified public purpose. Exchange Network assistance agreements allow recipients to develop infrastructure, systems and capacity to electronically report environmental information and participate fully on the Network. Applicants should identify and justify requests for the various structural elements available within their assistance agreement to best achieve their project goals. EPA will consider the following options for awarding EN resources:

- **Grant or Cooperative Agreement.** Grants represent direct funding to a recipient to support an identified project with defined environmental results. A cooperative agreement anticipates substantial involvement from EPA, in collaboration with the recipient, to achieve project results. If the recipient does not identify a preference, EPA's default award will be a grant.
- **Direct Funding or In-Kind Services.** EPA will consider grantee requests to use all or a portion of awarded grant funds to provide in-kind services to the recipient through an EPA contract vehicle. Applicants should request and justify project efficiencies they expect from this approach.

- **Single Grant or Performance Partnership/Consolidated Grants**. An applicant whose organization has an existing Performance Partnership Grant (PPG) with EPA may request any new grant recommended for funding be incorporated into the PPG. Similarly, a territorial applicant whose territory has a Consolidated Grant (CG) with EPA may request that new awards be incorporated into the CG. Absent a request from the recipient for inclusion within a PPG or CG, EPA will award the grant in a stand-alone vehicle.

## II-C. Funding Restrictions

Applicants may propose EN/EE project funding for costs associated with personnel salaries and fringe benefits, Intergovernmental Personnel Act Agreements (IPAs) travel, travel related to Exchange Network activities, equipment, supplies, contractual costs, in-kind services provided by EPA, and indirect costs. Applicants may *not* use EN/EE funding for the following functions (see Appendix K for definitions):

- **Construction costs;**
- **Operations and maintenance** including previously developed and implemented EN projects;
- **Workshops and Conferences** that are not initiated, advertised, and conducted for the benefit of the recipient and other state, tribal, territorial, or local representatives or public participants or are conducted primarily for EPA's benefit;
- **Pre-Award Costs** not previously requested to cover pre-award costs incurred 90 days or less before the award date; and
- **Management Fees** in excess of the direct costs and indirect costs at the rate approved by the applicant's cognizant audit agency, or at the rate provided for by the terms of the agreement negotiated with EPA.

# III. Eligibility Information

## III-A. Eligible Applicants

Eligible applicants for the Exchange Network Grant program include states, U.S. Territories (i.e., American Samoa, the Commonwealth of the Northern Mariana Islands, the District of Columbia, Guam, Palau, Puerto Rico, the U.S. Virgin Islands), federally recognized Indian tribes and native villages and inter-tribal consortia of federally recognized tribes (e.g., the Northwest Indian Fisheries Commission because their membership is primarily federally recognized tribes and they have sufficient controls to ensure tribes will benefit from funding).

---

***Examples of Eligible Project Leads:***

➢ State Department of Environmental Quality

➢ Territorial Environment Division

➢ Tribal Council on behalf of two or more tribal environmental and/or health agencies

➢ State Department of Public Health

➢ Tribal Water Quality Administration

➢ State Office of the Chief Information Officer

➢ Regional Air Quality Board delegated authority for the air program

➢ State university where the university or the university system is formally designated as an instrumentality of the state

---

Other entities, such as regional air pollution control districts and some public universities may apply for assistance if they are agencies or instrumentalities of a state under applicable state laws. These entities, as well as other entities that submit applications asserting they are agencies or instrumentalities of a state, must provide with the application a letter from the appropriate state Attorney General certifying that the applicant is an agency or instrumentality of the state. EPA will not consider an application that does not contain the required documentation. EPA recognizes that some EPA programs are delegated to local governments, which are responsible for reporting data to EPA. Local governments that can demonstrate that they are instrumentalities of the state by providing the documentation described in the preceding paragraph are eligible to apply for Exchange Network Grants. Most local governments that are delegated to implement EPA programs, however, are not agencies or instrumentalities of the state (i.e., a true agency or instrumentality is under the direct control of the state and the management of a state agency or instrumentality may generally be changed by the state executive or other state officials) and, therefore, are not eligible to apply. EPA encourages such entities to partner with a state applicant to allow for their data to be reported and shared through the Exchange Network. Interstate commissions and other interstate entities are not eligible to apply and are also encouraged to partner with a state applicant.

EPA will only evaluate applications from eligible entities (see above). EPA will notify ineligible applicants they are not being considered for funding within 15 calendar days of the ineligibility determination. Applicants with questions about eligibility can contact Salena Reynolds, Exchange Network Grants Program Manager, at (202) 566-0466 or reynolds.salena@epa.gov. They may also attend Exchange Network Users meetings to learn about and discuss Exchange Network projects and technology. Applicants not meeting the eligibility criteria may consider collaborative work with eligible organizations. EPA will only evaluate applications with eligible entities identified as the lead implementing agency for the project.

## III-B.  Threshold Criteria for Funding Goals

EPA will eliminate from consideration for funding any application that does not meet the following requirements for any of the Exchange Network grant-funding opportunities identified in this notice.

EPA will *only* review:

1.  Proposed goals that lead to the completion of activities listed in the Priorities Section (I-E), additional activities identified in Appendix A, or others provided they are consistent with EN or EE priorities. Completion in the context of the Exchange Network means committing to fully implement a flow, data publishing, deployment of a Web service or other eligible projects. Applicants should show their commitment to complete projects as one or more specific outputs. For E-Enterprise, completion means fully implementing an evaluation or assessment, developing findings and reaching conclusions or developing a target architecture or a "to-be" business process.

2.  Applications that comply with the application submission instructions and requirements in Section IV and Appendix D of this announcement. Section IV and Appendix D require that a project narrative not exceed 10 pages. EPA will not review any narrative page after the tenth page.

3.  Applications postmarked, delivered by an overnight courier service, or electronically submitted through www.grants.gov as specified in Section IV and Appendix D of this announcement on or before the application submission deadline published in Section IV and Appendix D of this announcement.

4.  Applications with project periods of no more than three years, applications from a single applicant with a maximum budget of $300,000 or multi-partner, collaborative applications with a maximum budget of $500,000.

5.  Applications from applicants with fewer than five active Exchange Network assistance agreements with the Agency. EPA will determine whether an applicant meets this threshold criterion on January 29, 2015, prior to the final scoring of applications by Agency grant review panels. EPA considers an assistance agreement active if the Agency has not yet approved the final technical report. EPA will consider an agreement closed (and therefore not included in this count), if the Regional Project Officer approves the applicant's final technical report on or before January 29, 2015.

EPA will *not* review:

1. Applications from applicants who already have five or more active Exchange Network assistance agreements with the Agency. EPA will determine whether an applicant meets this threshold criterion on January 29, 2015, prior to the final scoring of applications by Agency grant review panels. An assistance agreement will be considered active if EPA has not yet approved the final technical report. EPA will consider an agreement closed (and therefore not included in this count), if the Regional Project Officer approves the applicant's final technical report on or before January 29, 2015.

2. Applications with project periods of more than three years, applications from a single applicant with a budget of more than $300,000 or multi-partner, collaborative applications that have budgets over $500,000.

3. Applications from applicants who have unaddressed compliance issues with prior federal assistance agreements. Unaddressed compliance issues may include: open programmatic findings (programmatic baseline reporting), open administrative findings (administrative baseline reporting), high risk, or Inspector General audits. In order to be eligible for a new EN grant, the applicant must either: 1) Not have any issues identified in the IGMS Grantee Compliance and Database, or 2) Develop a Corrective Action Plan to address any issues identified in the IGMS Grantee Compliance Database, and have this Plan approved by the federal project officer.

4. Applications with any activities or deliverables for which the applicant has previously received funds. If a proposed goal is similar to one previously funded, the application must describe how previously funded activities differ from those currently proposed or how the current application will complement or build on past or ongoing work.

5. Applications postmarked, delivered by an overnight courier service, or electronically submitted through www.grants.gov after the submission deadline. These applications will be considered late and returned to the sender without further consideration unless the applicant can clearly demonstrate that it was late due to EPA mishandling or because of technical problems associated with www.grants.gov . Applicants should confirm receipt of their application with Salena Reynolds (reynolds.salena@epa.gov) as soon as possible after the submission deadline – failure to do so may result in EPA not reviewing the application.

6. Applications that include any ineligible tasks or activities. If an application is submitted that includes any ineligible tasks or activities, that portion of the application will be ineligible for funding and may, depending on the extent to which it affects the application, render the entire application ineligible for funding.

### III-C. Eligibility Criteria for Partnership Applications

EPA will consider the higher funding limit ($500,000) for projects that include more than one Exchange Network partner. EE applications must include more than one partner and are eligible for the $500,000 funding limit. For these, one eligible entity must lead the collaborative effort and assume program and financial responsibility for the project. In a letter of intent or similar document, partners must, state both their general support for the project, and commit to specific project activities. The lead partner must submit partner commitment documents with the application.

The lead partner for a partnership application must demonstrate within their application the project's support for the identified Exchange Network priorities and explain how the partnership components justify a need for additional partnership funding. **EPA will not consider partnerships formed from within a single state, territorial, or tribal government as eligible. For instance, a partnership between an environment and a health department within a state would not be an eligible partnership. EPA will limit funding for intrastate projects of this sort to the maximum funding for a single-jurisdiction grant for an Exchange Network application, which in FY 2015 is $300,000. Intra-state partnerships (unless it is a partnership between a state and a tribe) are not eligible for grants for the new EE related activities that are being incorporated into the EN program.**

### III-D. Cost Sharing or Matching

Grants for Exchange Network projects do not require cost sharing or matching of funds by applicants.

### IV. Application and Submission Information

Applicants for the FY 2015 Exchange Network Grant program must submit an application package to EPA by November 24, 2014. EPA will accept applications for National Environmental Information Exchange Network grants in one of two ways: 1) a hardcopy mailed or delivered application, including one original and two copies; or 2) an application submitted electronically through the grants.gov website. EPA will confirm receipt of each application with an e-mail to the contact(s) listed in the cover letter.

The specific requirements of the application package and each document included with the package are available in Appendix D, which outlines the format for the project narrative (no more than ten-single-spaced pages) and provides detailed application instructions. Appendix G provides a checklist of required documents to submit. Fillable versions of these forms are available at http://www.epa.gov/ogd/forms/forms.htm

EPA may require applicants approved for funding to submit additional or updated documents to complete the funding package. EPA will provide further instructions for submittal of additional or updated documents at that time.

### IV-A. Submission Date and Time

Signed and completed application packages as described in Appendix D must be sent electronically via grants.gov, postmarked, or delivered by an overnight courier service **no**

**later than 11:59 PM Eastern Standard Time, November 24, 2014**. EPA will return application packages to the sender without further consideration if they are postmarked, sent electronically through grants.gov or delivered by an overnight courier *after* the published closing date and time.

## IV-B. Intergovernmental Review

This funding opportunity is **not** subject to Executive Order (EO) 12372, "Intergovernmental Review of Federal Programs."

## IV-C. Partnership Agreements

EPA awards funds to one eligible applicant as the recipient even if other eligible applicants are partners or members of a coalition or consortium. The awardee is accountable to EPA for the proper expenditure of funds, programmatic and administrative reporting and attainment of program and environmental results.

Grantees may provide subgrants or subawards to fund partner work within the overall project, provided the recipient complies with applicable requirements for subawards or subgrants including those contained in 40 CFR Parts 30 or 31, as appropriate. Successful applicants cannot use subgrants or subawards to avoid requirements in EPA grant regulations for competitive procurement by using these instruments to acquire commercial services or products from for-profit organizations to carry out its assistance agreement. For more detailed information on partnership agreements, contracts and subawards, please see Appendix F.

EPA panels will review applicants' qualifications, past performance and reporting history and will consider, as appropriate and relevant, the qualifications, expertise and experience of formal partners. Applicants should detail their own project roles and responsibilities, experience and past performance and those of their formal partners. Section V, below, describes in detail the evaluation criteria and process EPA will use to make selections under this Notice.

## IV-D. Additional Provisions for Applicants Incorporated Into the Solicitation

Additional provisions that apply to this solicitation and/or awards made under this solicitation, including but not limited to those related to confidential business information, contracts and subawards under grants, and proposal assistance and communications, can be found at http://www.epa.gov/ogd/competition/solicitation_provisions.htm. These, and the other provisions that can be found at the website link, are important, and applicants must review them when preparing proposals for this solicitation. If you are unable to access these provisions electronically at the website above, please communicate with the EPA contact listed in this solicitation to obtain the provisions.

# V. Application Review Information

### V-A.1 Exchange Network Evaluation Criteria

Only eligible entities whose applications meet the threshold eligibility criteria in Section III of this announcement will be reviewed according to evaluation criteria set forth below. The EPA Selection Official will make final funding decisions based on an applicant's score and other factors discussed in section V-B.

EPA will score (highest possible score is 100) and rank applications. The possible point totals for each of the five major evaluation criteria are listed below in bold text. Sub-components (or possible point deductions) within each of the five criteria are listed in bold italic text below the relevant criterion.

### *Goals, Outputs, and Outcomes in Exchange Network Grant Applications*

**Each application must include one or more goals, outputs for each goal and at least one outcome for each goal.** Goals, outputs and outcomes each have specific meanings in the context of Exchange Network proposals. The following is a list of the Exchange Network usage for each of these terms.

- **Goals** are the products of a self-contained project such as the implementation of a dataflow. A proposed goal might be to upgrade eForms to use Shared CROMERR Services and Components, for instance. A proposed project must have at least one goal and may have more than one goal.

- Projects progress towards goals through a series of **outputs** from their beginning to their conclusion. Outputs are intermediate accomplishments necessary to achieve a particular goal. Examples include completion of a schema or testing a flow. Each output should have a scheduled completion date. Scheduled outputs demonstrate "a plan that allows the applicant to track, and report to EPA, progress towards achieving proposed goals" (see the second bulleted criterion on page 31).

- Each goal should have at least one **outcome** leading to an environmental result. Examples include supporting better decision-making by building data access for environmental professionals and the public or facilitating environmentally sound place-based decision-making through the inclusion of quality locational data. See section "I-D Environmental Results Supported by Assistance Activities" of this Solicitation Notice for more examples.

**If an applicant uses the terms "goals," "outputs" and "outcomes" properly, the application will be easier for reviewers to understand and score. Using terms such as "objective," "target," "task" or "milestone" will make it more difficult for reviewers to understand and properly score the application.**

Appendix E provides an example of how to demonstrate goals, outputs and outcomes clearly. EPA encourages applicants to follow this example when applying.

## 1. Project Outputs and Outcomes Leading to Environmental Results (20 points):

For each goal, EPA will use the following criteria to evaluate the appropriateness and clarity of project outputs and outcomes leading to environmental results (such as improved environmental decision-making):

- Does each proposed goal have at least one outcome that leads to an environmental result? These might include outcomes such as improving the timeliness, completeness, and accuracy of environmental data; reducing the burden and costs associated with data management and reporting; or supporting better environmental decision making by enhancing data access for environmental professionals and the public, as well as providing high quality locational data to facilitate place-based approaches such as community-oriented initiatives. *(10 points)*
- Does the application include a plan that allows the applicant to track and report progress towards achieving the proposed goal to EPA? Each grant-funded goal, such as a project to complete a web application that will allow users to display, analyze, or collect environmental information, should have **several outputs** scheduled over the project period. *(10 points)*

## 2. Project Feasibility and Approach (15 points):

EPA will evaluate the feasibility of proposed projects using the following criteria:

- Does the application clearly describe individual project roles and responsibilities for the applicant and, for collaborative projects, each partner? *(5 points)*
- All projects involving programmatic data must describe programmatic involvement in the development and management of the project. This description must include the names, positions and roles of all who are involved in the project. For example, "Jane Doe, multimedia inspector, will advise the Project Manager and contractor on the Compliance Dashboard design and take part in end user testing." Some projects may not need programmatic participants. An example would be a CROMERR system upgrade. In this case, the proposal should explain why programmatic involvement was unnecessary. *(5 points)*
- Applicants must explicitly commit, in their response to this Solicitation Notice, that they will reuse existing project-appropriate EN tools and resources. This requires searching Reusable Component Services (RCS) and Exchange Network Discovery Services (ENDS) for resources such as dataflows, Web services or EN services. The applicant must also commit in writing to register any new tool or resource they develop in RCS or any new node, dataflow or EN service in ENDS. For innovative flows, applicants must demonstrate that the project will result in reusable tools and services for the Exchange Network. Beginning in FY 2015 all applicants must commit to the following reuse and sharing outputs:
  - The applicant will search for, and use where appropriate, existing EN tools

and resources. This output would appear at or near the beginning of the project.

- The applicant will register any tool or resource they develop for the project. This output would appear at or near the end of the project. *(5 points)*

### 3. Exchange Network Priorities *(up to 30 points):*

EPA will evaluate the consistency of proposed work with EN priorities (Section I-E). More details on data exchange activities are in Appendix A or the EN website at http://www.exchangenetwork.net/exchanges/.

Applications will receive points for EN priorities only if the work plan commits to a completed and sustained product such as a data flow or a publishing effort.

For applications that have a single goal, the goal *must* commit to complete a project to be eligible for funding. For applications that have multiple goals, each goal must commit to complete a project. Any goal that is part of a multiple goal application that does not commit to complete a project will not be funded.

Under this criterion, projects that include at least one Tier 1 activity will receive the maximum 30 points. If an application is for a Tier 2 priority, and does not include any Tier 1 activities, it will only receive 20 points.

### 4. Budget, Resources, and Key Personnel (20 points):

EPA will evaluate: (1) the budget's appropriateness including the amount allocated to each goal and its adequacy to support and complete the proposed work; and (2) the qualifications of the project manager and other key personnel to perform the project.

- Does the application include a total budget amount for each goal in the project narrative? *(10 points)*
- Does the application document the qualifications of the project manager and other key personnel who would perform the proposed work? In the case of a tribal applicant who proposes to use a portion of this grant to hire key personnel for a capacity building proposal, has the applicant submitted a statement of knowledge, skills, abilities, and qualifications from the recruitment package for that position? *(5 points)*
- Expenditure of Awarded Grant Funds *(5 points)*
  Under this criterion, applicants will be evaluated based on their approach, procedures, and controls for ensuring that awarded grant funds will be expended in a timely and efficient manner.

**Failure to provide a detailed itemized budget will result in a mandatory 10-point deduction on your application.**

## 5. Past Performance (15 points):

EPA will evaluate the past performance of an Exchange Network grant applicant with one or more previous EN grants based on the percentage of semi-annual reports they have submitted historically.

- Has the applicant made sufficient progress toward achieving the expected results in the prior assistance agreements? *(10 points)*
- Has the applicant submitted at least 90% of the progress reports required in the terms and conditions of the prior assistance agreements within thirty days of their due dates? *(5 points)*

Please note that in evaluating applicants under this criterion, the Agency will consider the information provided by the applicant (including semi-annual report submissions) and may also consider relevant information from other sources (including agency files and prior or current grantors to verify or supplement the information supplied by the applicant).

EPA's monitoring of Exchange Network grant performance indicates that the majority of grantees are making steady progress. The work under some grants, however, is falling behind schedule or has stopped altogether. Although unliquidated obligations (ULO's – also known as unspent balances) are not a perfect indicator of grant progress, they can serve as a useful proxy to indicate if there are performance problems. Consequently, EPA established the following criteria for grants with excessively high ULO's or unspent balances:

**Figure 1-2: Criteria for Identifying Excessive ULO's**

| Period of Performance Milestone | Criteria – Unspent Balance as Percent of Awarded Funds |
|---|---|
| End of year two | Greater than or equal to 95 percent |
| End of year three | Greater than or equal to 70 percent |
| End of year four | Greater than or equal to 40 percent |
| End of year five | Greater than or equal to 10 percent |

The past performance evaluation criterion will include consideration of ULO's. Specifically, for any grant that meets the appropriate excessive ULO criterion in Figure 1-2, all applications submitted by the recipient of that grant will automatically lose 10 points, unless the applicant can explain that the excessively high ULO was not due to action or inaction on the part of the state, tribe or territory. For example, an adequate explanation would be delays in the grant's project schedule resulting from delays on the part of EPA. EPA will post lists of grants that meet these criteria on its Exchange Network website[10] during the first week of October 2014, and will also request that the Environmental Council of the States (ECOS) notify Exchange Network partners via an EN Alert. (Potential grant

---

[10] http://www.epa.gov/exchangenetwork/grants/

applicants may sign up for EN Alerts by sending a request to Greg McNelly of ECOS at gmcnelly@ecos.org ). The final determination of whether previously awarded Exchange Network grants meet the excessive ULO threshold will be made from the following quarter's report, which EPA will make available during January 2015.

### V-A.2  Evaluation Criteria for EN Projects that Relate to E-Enterprise

Only eligible entities whose applications meet the threshold eligibility criteria in Section III of this announcement will be reviewed according to evaluation criteria set forth below. The EPA Selection Official will make final funding decisions based on an applicant's score and other factors discussed in section V-B.

EPA will score (highest possible score is 100) and rank applications. The possible point totals for each of the five major evaluation criteria are listed below in bold text. Sub-components (or possible point deductions) within each of the five criteria are listed in bold italic text below the relevant criterion.

**1. Project Outputs and Outcomes Leading to Environmental Results (20 points):**

*Goals, Outputs, and Outcomes in Applications for E-Enterprise Related Activities*

**Each application must include one or more goals, outputs for each goal and at least one outcome for each goal.** Goals, outputs and outcomes each have specific meanings in the context of the proposals seeking funds for the EE related activities that are being incorporated into the EN program. The following is a list of the usage for each of these terms.

- **Goals** are the end products of a self-contained project such as the implementation of a streamlined or shared service. A proposed goal might be to share a common service across multiple agencies, for instance. A proposal must have at least one goal and may have more than one goal.

- Projects progress towards goals through a series of **outputs** from their beginning to their conclusion. Outputs are intermediate accomplishments necessary to achieve a particular goal. Examples include establishing a cloud-based software-as-a-service. Scheduled outputs should demonstrate "a plan that allows the applicant to track, and report to EPA, progress towards achieving proposed goals."

  Each goal should have at least one **outcome** leading to a result that streamlines a source environmental policy or the services for implementing that policy. Examples include reducing burden by harmonizing requirements for protecting confidential business information, and streamlining services by creating a shared financial assurance application.

Definitions of "outcome" and "output" may be found in Appendix K.

**If an applicant uses the terms "goals," "outputs" and "outcomes" properly, the application will be easier for reviewers to understand and score. Using terms such as "objective," "target," "task" or "milestone" will make it more difficult for reviewers to understand and properly score the grant application.**

Appendix E provides an example of how to demonstrate goals, outputs and outcomes clearly. EPA encourages applicants to follow this example when applying.

For each goal, EPA will use the following criteria to evaluate the appropriateness and clarity of project outputs and outcomes leading to environmental results (such as improved environmental decision-making):

- Does each proposed goal have at least one outcome that leads to a result that streamlines a source environmental policy or the services for implementing that policy? *(10 points)*
- Does the application include a plan that allows the applicant to track and report progress towards achieving the proposed goal to EPA? Each grant-funded goal, such as a shared service, should have several outputs scheduled over the project period. *(10 points)*

## 2. Project Feasibility and Approach (15 points):

EPA will evaluate the feasibility of proposed projects using the following criteria:

- Does the application clearly describe individual project roles and responsibilities for each partner? *(7.5 points)*
- All projects involving programmatic systems must describe programmatic involvement in the development and management of the project. This description must include the names, positions and roles of all who are involved in the project. For example, "Jane Doe, multimedia inspector, will advise the Project Manager and contractor on the Compliance Dashboard design and take part in end user testing." Some projects may not need programmatic participants. An example would be a system shared between two states. In this case, the proposal should explain why programmatic involvement was unnecessary. *(7.5 points)*

## 3. Alignment with E-Enterprise Priorities Being Incorporated into the EN Program (up to 30 points):

EPA will evaluate the consistency of proposed work with the E-Enterprise priorities that EPA is incorporating into the EN Program (Section I-E).

Applications will receive points for E-Enterprise related priorities only if the work plan commits to a completed and sustained product. For instance, if a project goal is to develop a shared service, there must be an output that commits grantee to full and sustained implementation of the project.

For applications that have a single goal, the goal *must* commit to complete a project to be eligible for funding. For applications that have multiple goals, each goal must commit to complete a project. Any goal that is part of a multiple goal application that does not commit to complete a project will not be funded.

Under this criterion, projects that include at least one Tier 1 activity will receive the maximum 30 points. If an application is for a Tier 2 priority, and does not include any Tier 1 activities, it will only receive 20 points.

### 4. Budget, Resources, and Key Personnel (20 points):

EPA will evaluate: (1) the budget's appropriateness including the amount allocated to each goal and its adequacy to support and complete the proposed work; and (2) the qualifications of the project manager and other key personnel to perform the project.

- Does the application include a total budget amount for each goal in the project narrative? *(10 points)*
- Does the application document the qualifications of the project manager and other key personnel who would perform the proposed work? In the case of a tribal applicant who proposes to use a portion of this grant to hire key personnel for a capacity building proposal, has the applicant submitted a statement of knowledge, skills, abilities, and qualifications from the recruitment package for that position? *(5 points)*
- Expenditure of Awarded Grant Funds *(5 points)*
  Under this criterion, applicants will be evaluated based on their approach, procedures, and controls for ensuring that awarded grant funds will be expended in a timely and efficient manner.

**Failure to provide a detailed itemized budget will result in a mandatory 10-point deduction on your application.**

### 5. Past Performance (15 points):

EPA will evaluate the past performance of a grant applicant with one or more previous EN grants based on the percentage of semi-annual reports they have submitted historically.

- Has the applicant made sufficient progress toward achieving the expected results in the prior assistance agreements? *(10 points)*
- Has the applicant submitted at least 90% of the progress reports required in the terms and conditions of the prior assistance agreements within thirty days of their due dates? *(5 points)*

Please note that in evaluating applicants under this criterion, the Agency will consider the information provided by the applicant (including semi-annual report submissions from previous Exchange Network grants) and may also consider relevant information from other sources (including agency files and prior or current grantors to verify or supplement the information supplied by the applicant).

## V-B.  Review and Selection Process

There will be one review panel for all EN proposals submitted to the Agency. All applications will first be evaluated against the threshold eligibility criteria listed in Section III of this announcement. Only those applications that satisfy all of the threshold eligibility criteria in Section III will be evaluated using the criteria listed above by the EPA review panel. The EPA review panel will then evaluate, score and rank EE related applications separately from EN applications for traditional Phase 2 or Phase 1 activities. The EPA review panel will base its evaluation, scoring and ranking of applications on the criteria listed in section V-A.1 for traditional EN applications, and Section V-A.2 for EE related applications. The EPA review panel will develop separate ranking lists for each program resulting from the evaluation reviews. Ranking lists and preliminary funding recommendations will then be submitted to the Selection Official, the Assistant Administrator of the Office of Environmental Information (OEI) or his or her designee, who will make the final funding decisions.

**Other Evaluation Factors:** Final funding decisions will be made by the Selection Official based on the rankings and preliminary recommendations of the EPA review panel. In making the final funding decisions, the EPA Selection official may consider one or more of the following factors:

- EPA programs' ability or readiness to support proposed project activities;
- Geographic distribution of funding;
- Selection of higher priority activities over other assistance activities;
- Ensuring participation in the Exchange Network by federally recognized Indian tribes and inter-tribal consortia; and
- EPA's capacity to provide any requested in-kind services.

## V-C.  Anticipated Award Dates

EPA anticipates that it will announce selection decisions in or around April 2015. EPA plans to issue the awards by July 2015.

# VI. Award Administration Information

## VI-A.  Award Notices

EPA will notify all applicants (by telephone, electronic or postal mail) of their status in or around April 2015. The notification will be sent to the original signer of the application or the project contact listed in the application. The notification of a full or partial funding recommendation, which advises the applicant that EPA has preliminarily selected and recommended their proposed project for award, is not an authorization to begin work. The award notice, signed by an EPA grants officer, is the authorizing document and will be provided through electronic or postal mail. The time between notification of selection and award of a grant can take up to 90 days or longer.

## VI-B.  Administration and National Policy Requirements

Each assistance agreement will include a set of Administrative Terms and Programmatic Conditions, such as requirements for electronic funding transfers, additional financial status reporting, limitations on payments to consultants and application of indirect cost rates. These terms and conditions form the basis for the final award of Exchange Network grant funding. Failure to concur with the included terms and conditions will invalidate the award.

In accordance with the Exchange Network Interoperability Policy, applicants must commit, in writing, to the reuse of existing dataflows and EN services registered in Exchange Network Discovery Services (ENDS), and other IT resources such as widgets and REST Web services registered in Reusable Component Services (RCS). For information on reuse, please see Appendix K. Applicants must also commit to registering any newly developed resources in ENDS or RCS as appropriate. Information about ENDS can be found at www.exchangenetwork.net/2011/07/15/exchange-network-discovery-service-ends/; information about RCS can be found at www.epa.gov/rcs. EPA will require all recipients of grants issued under this solicitation notice to meet these conditions.

EPA will include a grant condition in the assistance agreement requiring the recipient to submit a tailored Quality Assurance Project Plan (QAPP) to the EPA Regional Project Officer within 90 days of the award issuance date. This tailored QAPP must describe for each goal and task: the relevant task-specific Quality Assurance (QA) criteria, how the recipient will ensure adherence with the QA criteria, and how the recipient will confirm and document that the project deliverables meet the QA criteria. Completion of the Exchange Network Quality Assurance Reporting Form (QARF) satisfies the requirements for a tailored QAPP. The QA criteria information specified above must be documented for each goal and task under the Quality Assurance Measures section of the Exchange Network QARF. The template for the Exchange Network QARF can be found at http://www.epa.gov/exchangenetwork/grants/index.html and in Appendix I of this notice.

## VI-C.  Reporting

**Semi-Annual Performance Progress Reports:** Reporting is an important obligation that award recipients agree to undertake when they sign an assistance agreement. Both EPA and recipients are accountable to Congress and to the public for the proper and effective use of Exchange Network assistance funds. Award recipients will submit semi-annual and final technical reports electronically through EPA's Central Data Exchange (CDX) using a Web form. EPA will provide successful applicants with detailed instructions for registering with and reporting through CDX at the time of award.

## VI-D.  Dispute Resolution Provision

Assistance agreement competition-related disputes will be resolved in accordance with the dispute resolution procedures published in 70 FR (Federal Register) 3629, 3630 (January 26, 2005) which can be found at http://www.epa.gov/ogd/competition/resolution.htm. Copies of these procedures may also be requested by contacting Salena Reynolds at 202-566-0466 or reynolds.salena@epa.gov.

## VI-E.  Unliquidated Obligations

EPA expects an applicant that receives an award under this announcement to manage assistance agreement funds efficiently and effectively and make sufficient progress towards completing the project activities described in the work-plan in a timely manner. The assistance agreement will include terms and conditions implementing this requirement. EPA uses the criteria in section V-A to help determine if an applicant is expending grant funds at an acceptable rate. Grantees who meet the above criteria for excessive ULO's for Exchange Network assistance agreements may be subject to scoring penalties in future grant applications.

## VI-F. Additional Provisions for Applicants Incorporated Into the Solicitation

Additional provisions that apply to this solicitation and/or awards made under this solicitation, including but not limited to those related to DUNS, SAM, copyrights, disputes, and administrative capability, can be found at http://www.epa.gov/ogd/competition/solicitation_provisions.htm. These, and the other provisions that can be found at the website link, are important and applicants must review them when preparing proposals for this solicitation. If you are unable to access these provisions electronically at the website above, please communicate with the EPA contact listed in this solicitation to obtain the provisions.

## VII. Agency Contacts

The primary EPA Headquarters point of contact is:
        Salena Reynolds
        Exchange Network Grant Program Manager
        Office of Information Collection
        Office of Environmental Information
        Phone: (202) 566-0466
        Facsimile: (202) 566-1684
        Email: reynolds.salena@epa.gov

**Mailing Address**:
Salena Reynolds
U.S. Environmental Protection Agency
1200 Pennsylvania Avenue, NW (2823-T)
Washington, DC 20460

**Physical Address** *(for overnight, or courier deliveries)*:
Salena Reynolds
U.S. Environmental Protection Agency
1301 Constitution Avenue, NW (Rm 6416S)
Washington, DC 20004

# Appendix A

## Suggested Exchange Network Data Exchange Activities

This Appendix outlines some example project opportunities that applicants should consider when applying for the FY 2015 National Environmental Information Exchange Network Grant Program. Appendix A contains two subsections: *I.) Definition of Standard Milestones for EPA Information System or Data Exchanges*; and *II.) Data Exchanges* (descriptions of individual data exchanges and related EN activities). This Appendix highlights the EPA Program Office activities related to flows and provides suggested activities for applicants to consider when developing their application.

The Exchange Network Grant Program supports a variety of activities, including the development of common data standards, formats and trading partner agreements for sharing data over the Exchange Network and implementation of collaborative, innovative uses of the Exchange Network. It also supports the standardization, exchange and integration of geospatial information to address environmental, natural resource and related human-health issues.

As part of the standardization mentioned above, grantees must utilize data standards that have been previously approved by the Exchange Network Leadership Council (ENLC) as they develop Exchange Network products and services. In most cases, the data standards needed in implementation will have previously been incorporated in the major EPA systems and Exchange Network dataflows. These data standards can simply be re-used. For detailed information on each ENLC approved standard please refer to the Exchange Network website at http://www.exchangenetwork.net/standards/index.htm. There is also a separate document (located at the website cited above) to assist you with understanding how these standards have been implemented within the specific EPA systems. Please note that in some cases applicants may need to identify areas for new data standardization. If so, applications should identify the data standards needed and project the funding required to development them.

The success of the Exchange Network will ultimately depend on how EPA and its partners use the data and information that are exchanged to enhance decision-making and programmatic operations. EPA encourages all partners to use the Exchange Network to meet their business needs. This could include exchanging data that supports national environmental systems, as well as data that support particular state, territorial and tribal needs. Innovative projects must demonstrate that they will leverage Exchange Network technology and result in the development of reusable services for the Exchange Network. These reusable services and components must be registered into the Exchange Network Discovery Service (ENDS) and into the Reusable Component Services (RCS), as appropriate.

# I. Definition of Standard Milestones for EPA Information Systems or Data Exchanges

This section will assist EPA Programs and Exchange Network partners in better understanding the EPA Program Office activities and establish consistency across all dataflows by further defining each milestone. These activities may be already completed, in process or planned at the time of release of this guidance.

**Testing of XML schema - (Version X)** - Schema has completed EPA testing and is ready for limited release to Exchange Network Partners that will support the testing process with EPA to identify any potential issues from real data exchanges. This includes the use of real data sets in XML instance documents. At this stage, Partners will have the constructs for mapping data to their own systems and sufficient time would be needed by these partners to complete that process once the schema(s) is released.

**Release of final XML schema – (Version X)** - Schema has undergone conformance review and is ready for posting to the Exchange Network website for access by all Exchange Network Partners (www.exchangenetwork.net).

**National database available for testing** - National database is ready for testing to exchange data in a format that complies with agreed upon standards and rules. For example, the database can support testing the receipt and processing of XML instance documents or a converted format as part of the exchange process.

**Availability of EPA node services for testing** - EPA Node services include all central services the program offices need or choose that enable a more efficient data exchange among exchange partners. Examples include XML validation (Schema and Schematron), Network Authentication and Authorization Service (NAAS), XML Gateway services, and the Universal Description and Discovery Integration tool.

**Readiness for complete end-to-end testing by Exchange Network partners** - At this stage, the XML schema(s) at a minimum are ready for testing by Network Partners and the National Database and EPA Node services are available for testing. In addition, all EPA accounts have been established for testing (e.g. privileges to NAAS and authorization to the database)

**Flow Configuration Document completed or updated** - Flow Configuration Documents identify and standardize the minimum information needed by trading partners to execute a data exchange. They describe the technical configuration and business processes used to exchange data between trading partners.

**System ready to receive or publish** - This status indicates that a sufficient amount of end-to-end testing has occurred and all problems have been addressed, the XML schema(s) has been released, supporting documentation has been finalized, all production readiness reviews have been completed, the Program Office has received approval (if applicable) from the National Computing Center for deploying new code to production, and the appropriate parties (e.g. helpdesks) have been notified of release and have the necessary tools to support Exchange Network Partners' inquiries.

## II. Data Exchanges

This section of Appendix A describes the individual data exchanges (and related Network activities) for which EPA is soliciting FY 2015 Exchange Network grant applications. It is organized by media and includes both Phase 1 and Phase 2 data exchanges and related activities. As the Exchange Network community is actively engaged in Phase 2, EPA has adjusted priorities for this grant solicitation to support those activities and dataflows. This includes placing a higher (Tier 1) priority on data publishing and access applications and tools, virtual sharing, virtual node implementation support, shared CROMERR services and components, and implementation of new and innovative dataflows.

Each individual data exchange is described below and includes additional activities applicants should consider for their proposals. Those activities must align with EPA's programmatic priorities in Section I-E and will be scored according to the tiering in that section.

The data exchange descriptions highlight programmatic milestones and potential activities for each exchange during the FY 2015-2018 timeframe. Applicants can propose to implement one or more of these data exchanges, which are organized by media:

## Other Data Exchanges

# Air Quality System (AQS)

**Description:**

AQS is the official EPA repository of ambient air quality monitoring data, and related location and measurement metadata, collected by state, tribal, and local governments. It is used for regulatory purposes to determine compliance with the Clean Air Act, and for scientific and health effects research. Presently the state, local, and tribal agencies are submitting data to AQS using version 2.2a of the AQS flow. This flow was updated in 2012 to support automated processing of submitted data, but no changes were made to the AQS XML schema.

40 CFR Part 58 Appendix A defines a number of monitoring QA/QC assessments that do not map cleanly into the data elements of AQS or the version 2.2a XML schema. In 2014, EPA redesigned how AQS accepts, processes, and reports QA/QC data. Additionally, EPA updated the monitor metadata utilized by AQS to more closely reflect 40 CFR Part 58 requirements. To incorporate these changes, the AQS flat file transaction format was revised and the AQS XML schema was updated to version 3.0. The changes support the additional data elements and outdated elements were dropped.

| Exchange Network Program Office Activities | |
|---|---|
| **Milestone** | **Target Completion** |
| EPA finalization of information content additions for XML schema | Complete |
| Draft AQS XML Schema v.3.0 | Complete |
| Final AQS XML Schema v.3.0 | Complete |
| Update to AQS Flow Configuration Document v.3.0 | Complete |
| Availability of AQS staging environment for testing v.3.0 | Complete |
| Availability of AQS production system for v.3.0 submissions | 09/30/2014 |

All submitters must use the revised flat file format or XML Schema v3.0 to submit data collected in 2015 and beyond. That is, data measured in 2014 but reported in 2015 may be in the current formats, but data collected (e.g., with a sample/measurement date) in 2015 must be in the new format. *(Tier 2)*

### Additional Activities to be considered by Grant Applicants
1. Upgrade of reporting agency's IT infrastructure to allow end-to-end use of XML format for ambient air quality monitoring data. *(Tier 2)*
2. Development of re-useable tools for data quality screening of ambient air quality measurement data (i.e. identification of statistical outliers and anomalies, collect audit and performance assessment (QA/QC) data from independent agencies and compare it to / merge it with your sample data, etc.) *(Tier 2)*

*Note:* *All activities are eligible for funding provided that the project proposal includes a commitment to deploy the dataflow into production.*

# Emission Inventory System (EIS)

**Description:**

The Emissions Inventory System (EIS) is the system for storing all current and historical emissions inventory data. It will be used to receive and store emissions data and generate annual and triennial National Emission Inventory beginning with the 2008 NEI.

The National Emissions Inventory (NEI) is EPA's compilation of estimates of air pollutants discharged on an annual basis and their sources. EPA uses the NEI to track emissions trends over time, develop regional pollutant reduction strategies, set and analyze regulations, perform air toxics risk assessments including inhalation risks and multi-pathway exposure, model air pollutant dispersion and deposition, and measure environmental performance as required by the Government Performance and Results Act.

**Additional Activities to be considered by Grant Applicants:**

EIS reporting will make use of a schema that is expected to shorten the length of time required to meet reporting deadlines, and reduce burden on state, local and tribal agencies through the use of the Consolidated Emission Reporting schema (CERS). The CERS facilitates the reporting of data from state/local/tribal agencies-to-EPA for the NEI. Although all states are reporting to EIS through the Exchange Network, most regional and local air pollution control authorities are not because they are not eligible for Exchange Network grants. Therefore, EPA suggests that states partner with local governments delegated to report to EIS to transition reporting from legacy methods to the Exchange Network, (Tier 2)

In addition to the submission of emissions data to the EIS, grant applicants may also apply for funds to:

1. Improve access to environmental information for environmental program staff, managers, the public and other stakeholders.
2. Support the sharing of data among EN partners, especially cross-state, cross-tribal, or state-tribal data exchanges
3. Support the transition from locally installed nodes to the EPA hosted Virtual Node.

# Radon Data Exchange

## Description:

Radon remains a leading cause of cancer. EPA, states, tribes and several national and regional consortia all collect radon data. These programs have differing data needs, reporting requirements, thresholds, calculation protocols and approaches to validation and verification of data.

Despite these differences, each of these data collections share the common purpose of improved tracking and understanding of radon exposure. Data are information and information is the programmatic foundation for effective radon risk reduction. The people leading these programs need access to data that are reliable, consistent, flexible and comparable across programs. While a significant amount of radon data exists today, there are currently no systems that allow for the examination of data from multiple sources or to draw larger conclusions about radon at a regional or national level. Exchange Network partners have an opportunity to use the Network to improve access to radon data and promote better management of exposure risks.

The New Jersey Department of Environmental Quality has developed an XML schema and a set of Web services for publishing radon data that are securely consumed by their state's Health Department. This model can be replicated in other states using the resources that New Jersey created. More information on these resources, including the XML schema and Flow Configuration Document, is available at http://www.exchangenetwork.net/data-exchange/radon/ .

The majority of the data included in NJ's database are similar to that identified as "core radon data elements" by the Radon State Data Exchange work group. EPA is interested in working with other radon stakeholders through this work group to build the capacity to share radon data via Web services. Visit http://www.radonleaders.org/exchange/ for more information about the Radon State Data Exchange work group.

## Activities to be considered by Grant Applicants:

- Participate in the Radon State Data Exchange Work Group to discuss radon data exchange needs and collaboratively coordinate on implementing standardized Web services.
- Evaluate the Radon XML schema previously created by the New Jersey Department of Environmental Quality.
- Map radon data to the Radon XML schema and build the capacity to generate and share those XML files via Network Web services.
- Implement Exchange Network Web services that make radon test data available to other stakeholders and the public as appropriate.

These activities are eligible for funding as Tier 1 priorities provided that the proposal commits to implementing the Web services that provide access to Radon data.

# ICIS
## Integrated Compliance Information System

**Description:**

ICIS, the modernized version of the Permit Compliance System (PCS) and the Air Facility System (AFS), supports NPDES wastewater discharge program functions (e.g., permitting, compliance monitoring, enforcement, and special regulatory programs), as well as air stationary source compliance and enforcement data. ICIS accepts XML-formatted submissions of NPDES and air data from States, Tribes and local environmental agencies via the Exchange Network. The ICIS exchange will be completed with the release of the ICIS-Air Electronic Data Transfer (EDT) implementation of the system in October 2014.

The ICIS electronic submission implementation was accomplished in four parts:

- **Part 1**: Batch DMR for NPDES Hybrid States. As of May 2008, *Hybrid States* were able to electronically transfer (batch) their DMR data from their state system to ICIS–NPDES and directly enter all of their non-DMR NPDES data into ICIS–NPDES via the ICIS Web screens. Hybrid states typically use ICIS-NPDES to directly manage their NPDES program.

- **Part 2**: NetDMR. As of June 2009, ICIS-NPDES became capable of receiving DMRs (via CDX) from facilities that had electronically signed and submitted them using NetDMR. The NetDMR tool was developed pursuant to an Exchange Network grant managed by Texas with the participation of 11 other states, OEI and OECA. The DMR XML schema components developed in Part 1: Batch DMR for Hybrid States formed the basis for the NetDMR flow. NetDMR currently supports more than 14 States and 8 EPA Regions.

- **Part 3:** Full Batch NPDES States. As of December 2012, Full Batch states that have their own systems to manage the NPDES program were able to electronically transfer (batch) some or all of their NPDES data from their state systems via CDX to ICIS-NPDES.

- **Part 4 :** Air EDT Delegated Agencies. State, tribe and local agencies t h a t have their own systems to manage the air program were able to electronically transfer some or all of their air compliance data from their own systems via CDX to ICIS-Air.

### Activities to be Considered by Grant Applicants:

ICIS grant applicants should consider the following activities among their opportunities for obtaining grant funding:
- Extract and convert the data from State NPDES and air systems into the XML format needed to submit data to ICIS electronically.
- Modify state systems to accommodate the data requirements for ICIS-NPDES and ICIS-Air.

- Install and configure ICIS-NPDES and ICIS-Air plug-ins available on the Exchange Network.

ICIS-Air activities are eligible for funding as Tier 1 priorities. ICIS-NPDES activities are eligible for funding as Tier 2 priorities. Proposals for both are eligible for funding provided that the proposal commits to putting a new data family flow into production.

# ICIS Data Publishing

**Description:**

ICIS supports NPDES wastewater discharge program functions (e.g., permitting, compliance monitoring, enforcement, and special regulatory program), as well as Air stationary source compliance and enforcement data. ICIS accepts XML-formatted submissions of NPDES and Air data from states, tribes and local environmental agencies via the Exchange Network. The ICIS exchange will be completed with the final release of the Air Electronic Data Transfer (EDT) implementation of ICIS-Air in October 2014.

States hosting their own NPDES and Air systems may have requirements to have their data in ICIS published back to them so they can consume it for various purposes, including performing quality assurance. In addition, states hosting their own electronic DMR (eDMR) systems may need to have ICIS limit data published back to them to derive anticipated DMRs or ICIS reference code table data that has been recently changed. They could then consume this data for accurate mapping in subsequent data submissions to ICIS.

The ICIS data publishing flow enables states to extract new and changed reference table data as well as new and changed NPDES and Air data contained in EPA's ICIS system. OECA's planned milestones in enabling data access and publishing are shown below.

| Exchange Network Program Office Activities | |
| --- | --- |
| **Milestone** | **Target Completion** |
| Data Access Integrated Project Team (IPT) initiated. | Completed |
| Production release of Web services to extract recently changed data from seven ICIS reference tables. | Completed |
| Draft release of Web services to extract recently changed state data from basic permit, pretreatment permit, limit, discharge monitoring report (DMR), narrative condition, compliance schedule, compliance monitoring, and enforcement action ICIS-NPDES data families. | Completed |
| Pilot states test draft Web services to extract recently changed state data from basic permit, pretreatment permit, limit, discharge monitoring report (DMR), narrative condition, compliance schedule, compliance monitoring, and enforcement action data. | Completed |
| Production release of Web services to extract recently changed state data from basic permit, pretreatment permit, limit, discharge monitoring report (DMR), narrative condition, compliance schedule, compliance monitoring, and enforcement action ICIS-NPDES data families. | Completed |

| | |
|---|---|
| Draft release of Web services to extract recently changed state data from general permit, permit component, unpermitted facility, tracking event, violation and program report ICIS-NPDES data families. | Completed |
| Pilot states test draft Web services to extract recently changed state data from general permit, permit component, unpermitted facility, tracking event, violation and program report data. | August 2014 |
| Production release of Web services to extract recently changed state data from general permit, permit component, unpermitted facility, tracking event, violation and program report ICIS-NPDES data families. | August 2014 |
| Draft release of Web services to extract recently changed State, Tribal and Local Agency Air compliance and enforcement data from ICIS-Air data families. | January 2015 |
| Pilot states test draft Web services to extract recently changed State, Tribal and Local Agency Air compliance and enforcement data. | March 2015 |
| Production release of Web services to extract recently changed State, Tribal and Local Agency Air compliance and enforcement data from ICIS-Air data families. | May 2015 |

**Activities to be Considered by Grant Applicants:**

ICIS data publishing grant applicants should consider the following activities among their opportunities for obtaining grant funding:

- Review the XML Schema files developed under the IPT work and assist the IPT with the testing of the schema files.
- Develop requirements and design for the capability of invoking the Web services to extract data out of ICIS via CDX and import the data to the State, Tribal or Local Agency database.
- Develop and implement data mappings and the capability of invoking the Web services to extract data out of ICIS via CDX and import the data to the State, Tribal or Local database.
- Create the ability on the state side to consume ICIS reference code table data and other NPDES or Air data in XML format and use it for their individual State, Tribal or Local needs.

- Create the ability on the state side to consume ICIS-NPDES limit data for use in deriving anticipated DMRs in XML format into their individual state eDMR systems.

These activities when proposed for ICIS-Air are eligible for funding as Tier 1 priorities provided that the proposal commits to putting the services that consume ICIS data into production. When proposed for ICIS-NPDES are eligible as Tier 2 priorities.

# NetDMR Electronic Reporting Tool

## Description:

Electronic transmission of discharge monitoring reports (DMRs) allows NPDES permitting authorities to get out of the business of printing and mailing hard copy paper DMR forms to thousands of facilities, sorting the paper forms received, keypunching results by hand, and filing the paper forms. The National Installation of NetDMR has been developed collaboratively among a group of states (led by Texas), OECA and OEI to be a common, centrally-hosted electronic DMR application closely integrated with EPA's ICIS-NPDES system. The Central Data Exchange (CDX) is used for the exchange of data between NetDMR and ICIS-NPDES.

Version 1.0 of the National Installation of NetDMR was released for use by permittees of select pilot states and EPA Regions in June 2009. Version 1.5 of NetDMR, released in January of 2013, now supports more than fourteen states and eight EPA Regions, and additional instances can be created.

States that have specific business reasons why an instance within the National Installation of NetDMR cannot meet their programmatic requirements may wish to develop and deploy an alternative electronic DMR (eDMR) system within their state environment. State-hosted eDMR systems can be used to ensure timely and accurate reporting of DMRs by permittees to the regulatory authority and EPA's ICIS-NPDES system, using CDX and the Exchange Network.

## Activities to be Considered by the Grant Applicants:

The 2015 Exchange Network grant process will support efforts by states, in consultation with their EPA Regions, to: pilot test and launch their instances within the National Installation of NetDMR (Area 1); or develop, test, and implement their own eDMR system (Area 2).

*Area 1 – Testing and Implementation of State Instance within NetDMR National Installation*

Effective implementation includes development of all the business processes to move from a paper-based system to an electronic system, with the understanding that a paper-based system may need to be maintained for several years until all permittees are converted to the electronic system. Applicants could describe the efforts needed by the state to effectively test and launch the use of their instance within the National Installation of NetDMR, and discuss their adoption rate goals and milestones. Applications could also assist states in converting from paper to electronic processes, ensuring that Subscriber Agreements are properly handled according to CROMERR requirements, and ensuring that permit limits are up to date in ICIS-NPDES. Applicants could identify specific production implementation dates that the state prefers for their implementation within the National Installation of NetDMR.

*Area 2 – Development, Testing and Implementation of eDMR System within a State Environment*

Some states have specific business reasons why an instance within the National Installation of NetDMR cannot meet their programmatic requirements; thus they need an alternative eDMR system. For states with these requirements, this area can provide support for technical activities that lead to successful implementation of an eDMR system within the state environment. In these cases, applicants might explain why it is advantageous to develop and deploy a stand-alone system (which requires state operation and maintenance). Applicants could discuss costs and milestones associated with deploying and testing the application to ensure it works properly and sends required data to ICIS-NPDES using the approved schema and methodology.

*Note: Under either area the grantee could indicate whether the state plans to mandate electronic submission of DMRs for permits that are renewed after the project is completed. Additionally, these activities are eligible for funding as **Tier 2** priorities provided that the project proposal commits to deploying the NetDMR instance or the eDMR system into production.*

## Electronic Reporting of Notices of Intent (eNOI) and Special Regulatory Program Reports

**Description:**

Providing a means for members of the regulated community to submit NPDES data to EPA and states electronically by filling out an online Notice of Intent (NOI) form or special regulatory program report online allows state permitting authorities to transition away from entering thousands of permits and reports by hand and storing paper forms.

OECA is in the process of promulgating an Electronic Reporting Rule (NPDES eReporting Rule) that proposes to make the regulated community's electronic reporting of NPDES data mandatory. In preparation, OECA has developed a national electronic reporting tool called the NPDES e-Reporting Tool (NeT) for the regulated community to use in filing electronic NOIs. NeT is designed to capture this data and populate the ICIS-NPDES system with general permit covered facility permits and their associated limit data. Ultimately, the tool may include the ability to electronically capture and store CAFO, biosolid, CSO event, annual pretreatment, SSO event, industrial user compliance, and MS4 storm water program report information from the regulated community.

NeT creates XML files and submits them to ICIS-NPDES based upon the schema developed under the ICIS-NPDES Full Batch Integrated Project Team (IPT). CROMERR compliant Central Data Exchange (CDX) services are used for NeT's user registration process, handling of user account information, digital signature, copy of record (COR) storage, and submission of data to ICIS-NPDES through the Exchange Network. States will be able to host their own NOI forms in EPA's NeT for electronic reporting and retrieve their eNOI form data from CDX to save on their development, hosting, and maintenance costs.

In addition, states may want to consider creating and hosting their own NPDES eReporting tools for their regulated community to use. State-hosted NPDES eReporting systems developed under this effort must ensure timely and accurate data from the regulated community are transferred to EPA's ICIS-NPDES system using CDX and the Exchange Network in an XML format that matches the existing schema developed under the ICIS-NPDES Full Batch IPT.

| Exchange Network Program Office Activities | |
|---|---|
| **Milestone** | **Target Completion** |
| Production release of NeT eReporting tool to support EPA Region 6's Gulf of Mexico master general permit NOIs for Offshore Oil Drillers | Completed |
| Production release of Office of Water Regional Storm Water Multi-Sector General Permit NOI and annual report forms within NeT | October 2014 |
| Proposed deadline* for electronic reporting of all other state NOIs and special regulatory program report data to EPA | June 2016 |

\* Note: deadline is included within EPA's proposed NPDES eReporting Rule and is subject to change depending on final promulgation of the Rule.

**Activities to be Considered by the Grant Applicants:**

The 2015 Exchange Network grant process could support efforts by states, in consultation with their EPA Regions, to: pilot test and launch their electronic NOI and special regulatory report forms and processes within OECA's NeT electronic reporting tool (Area 1); develop, test, and implement their own NOI and program report electronic reporting system (Area 2); or modify their existing electronic reporting system to align with forthcoming requirements of the proposed NPDES Electronic Reporting Rule (Area 3).

*Area 1 – Test and Implementation of State Forms and Business Processes within OECA's NPDES e-Reporting Tool (NeT)*

Effective implementation often requires development of all the business processes to move from a paper-based system to an electronic system, with the understanding that a paper-based system will need to be maintained for several years until all permittees are converted to the electronic system. Applicants could describe the efforts needed by the state to effectively define business process flows, test and launch the use of their notices of intent and program reports within NeT, and discuss their adoption rate goals and milestones. Applicants could also assist in converting from paper to electronic processes, ensuring that Subscriber Agreements are properly handled according to CROMERR requirements, and ensuring that permit limits are up to date in ICIS-NPDES. Applicants could identify specific production implementation dates that the state prefers for their implementation within NeT.

*Area 2 – Development, Testing and Implementation of a NPDES Electronic Reporting System within a State Environment*

Some states have specific business reasons why hosting their general permit NOI forms within OECA's NeT tool cannot meet their programmatic requirements; thus they need an alternative eReporting system. For states with more specific state requirements, this area can provide support for technical activities that lead to successful implementation of an NOI and special regulatory program report eReporting system within the state environment. In these cases, applicants might explain why it is advantageous to develop and deploy their own system (which requires state operation and maintenance). Applicants could discuss costs and milestones associated with deploying and testing the application to ensure it works properly and sends required data to ICIS-NPDES using the approved schema and methodology.

*Area 3 – Upgrade of State System to Meet Requirements of EPA's NPDES Electronic Reporting Rule*

This area provides support for states to modify their state systems to ensure that they can capture, store, and transmit to EPA any new data that will become required under Appendix

A of 40 CFR 127 when the proposed NPDES eReporting Rule becomes final. Applicants could discuss the costs and milestones associated with upgrading their state system to ensure it can send the required data to ICIS-NPDES using the approved schema and methodology. Activities under areas 1 and 2 are eligible for funding as Tier 1 priorities, provided that the applicant proposes to deploy the project's output (e.g., system, business process). Activities under area 3 are eligible for funding as a Tier 2 priority, provided that the applicant complete and deploys the upgrade.

**Resource Conservation and Recovery Act
Information
(RCRAInfo)**

**Description:**

RCRAInfo is a national, Web-based system which provides data entry, data management, and data reporting functions used to support the implementation and oversight of the Resource Conservation and Recovery Act (RCRA) of 1976 and the Hazardous and Solid Waste Amendments (HSWA) of 1984 as administered by EPA (through its Regions) and authorized States. RCRAInfo identifies and categorizes hazardous waste handlers, and includes high quality information about regulated activities, permit/closure status, compliance with Federal and State regulations, and cleanup activities. Only those that are a delegated authority under RCRA Subtitle C can submit data to RCRAInfo, however, non-delegated states or tribes can receive data from RCRAInfo via RCRAInfo outbound services. EPA encourages recipients to evaluate and explore the use of outbound Web services and to partner with EPA to identify outbound service needs and requirements. Additionally, States that are currently performing double-data entry should seek to use either RCRAInfo inbound or outbound services to eliminate that double- data entry.

| Exchange Network Program Office Activities | |
|---|---|
| Milestone | Target Completion |
| User Specified Outbound Services | As requested |
| Supportive Outbound Services | As requested |
| RCRAInfo upgrade/enhancements including schema revision | 12/2015 |

**Additional Activities to be considered by Grant Applicants**

Participants are encouraged to develop innovative ways for interacting with RCRAInfo Data including mobile application to be used "in the field."

*Note: This activity is eligible for funding as a **Tier 1** activity provided that the project plan commits to deploying a production application that consumes RCRAInfo outbound services*

# Open Dump Data Exchange

## Description:

The Open Dump problem facing tribes is immense and badly in need of inventorying the universe of the problem. The EPA's Office of Resource Conservation and Recovery (ORCR) and the DOI-Indian Health Service (IHS) all need updated and timely information on Open Dumps on Indian Country. The Exchange Network is in a unique position to assist and promote the timely, accurate sharing of key information on Open Dumps to a vast set of partners. This is a data set that has even OMB's attention. Development of specific data standards might be needed. Development or enhancement of the Fac ID 3.0 schema might fit the data exchange needs of this dataflow. However, a new schema might be necessary for the dataflow. Tribes are encouraged to develop the data requirements that will meet ORCR and IHS data needs and develop the appropriate schema and flow configuration to meet these data needs.

## Milestones:
- Test existing Schema found at http://www.exchangenetwork.net/data-exchange/open-dump-data-exchange/
- Develop Web services
- Complete end to end testing by tribes with CDX
- Flow configuration document completed
- Convene an IPT on the dataflow
- Mentor other tribes on the dataflow

## Additional Activities to be considered by Grant Applicants:

Integrated Project Team involvement is encouraged to assist in building out the schema for Open Dumps. Defining, vetting and building a comprehensive standard set of Web Services for Open Dump dataflow would advance the Network and serve as a model for other data service publishing. Documenting the dataflow is needed.

*Note: This activity is eligible for funding as a Tier 1 activity provided that the project plan commits to putting the Open Dump data exchange into production.*

# eBeaches

## Description:

eBeaches is the electronic data transmission system that allows EPA to securely receive and display state beach water quality and swimming advisory data two hours after state and local agencies send the data. eBeaches supports the Beaches Environmental Assessment and Coastal Health (BEACH) Act requirement to collect, store, and display beach public right-to-know pollution occurrence data. States should submit spatial representations of the beaches reported in the Beach Notification (PRAWN) and monitoring stations in Beach Monitoring (WQX) submissions using the NHDEvent dataflow.

## Activities and Suggestions to be considered by Grant Applicants:

Applicants should consider the following steps prior to data submissions.
- Read all support documentation at http://www.epa.gov/waterscience/beaches/grants/datausers/index.htm *(This activity is not eligible for funding)*
- Consider publishing Beach closure data in real time, even though the EPA currently updates data on a two-hour cycle. *(tier 2)*
- Map systems to the approved national XML schemas. http://www.exchangenetwork.net/communities-of-interest/water/ *(Tier 2\*)*
- Implement NHDEvent dataflow for BEACON beach locations to be geo-referenced to the NHD. Link beach locations consistent with the NHD and the Geospatial One Stop Hydrography Standard. *(Tier 2\*)*
- Verify in WQX/STORET organization name (org_id) to sample station (station_id) to beach name (project _id aka beach_id and national project id (EPABEACH) relationship/links to ensure correct stations are linked to corresponding beach. *(Tier 2\*)*
- Check with other internal state offices for existing Node capability and EPA virtual node access before developing Node capability for each beach dataflow. *(This activity is not eligible for funding)*
- Validate XML instance documents prior to submission via CDX (node or ENSC). *(Tier 2\*)*
- Participate in biweekly/monthly Beach conference calls. *(this activity is not eligible for funding)*

*\*Applications will be scored as Tier 2 proposals provided that this is a new dataflow for the applicant and that the project proposal commits to deploying the eBeaches dataflow into production.*

# Safe Drinking Water Information System (SDWIS)

**Description:**

SDWIS State is an EPA-provided system designed to assist primacy agencies in managing their Public Water System Supervision (PWSS) programs under the Safe Drinking Water Act (SDWA). Currently, SDWA data flows use XML files to exchange data between the Primacy Agency's SDWIS State system (or other PWSS program management system) and EPA for quarterly reporting and between other stakeholders, such as laboratories and other state agency systems and state agencies. EPA is in the process of replacing SDWIS State with a new system, SDWIS Primacy Agency (or "SDWIS Prime)[11]. EPA plans to replace SDWIS State with SDWIS Prime by May 31, 2015.

Whereas SDWIS State relied on XML (and other format) files for data transfer, SDWIS Prime will leverage secure, ReSTful Web services for data exchange. Many primacy agencies have other, external business systems that leverage Open Database Connectivity (ODBC) for implementing data exchanges with SDWIS State. As SDWIS Prime will be housed in a secure "cloud" environment accessible from the web, these ODBC connections are insecure and should be replaced by calls to secure Web services. At this time, the SDWIS Prime project team has identified a number of candidate Web services and development is underway.

In addition, the SDWIS Prime project team is planning the release of a Compliance Monitoring Data Portal (CMDP) January 31, 2015. CMDP will be accessible from the Exchange Network and will be a single, authoritative, CROMERR compliant collection site for laboratory samples data and public water system information updates and operating status reports. CMDP will "route" submissions to the appropriate primacy agency system or to SDWIS Prime for further action. More details of how the CMDP will operate will be available in October-November 2014.

**Additional Activities to be considered by Grant Applicants:**

**Tier 1 Activities:**

**Collaborative Opportunity:** partnership application consisting of multiple state, territorial and tribal partners working to share drinking water data with and between other state, tribal, territorial, and federal agencies/organizations using ReSTful Web services that consume SDWIS Prime data.

Adding functionality to the Compliance Monitoring Data Portal (CMDP - anticipated first release date mid-FY 2015) to address additional features requested by states, submitting laboratories, and utilities. Initial CMDP development is funded by an earlier EN grant awarded to a group of states. However, the original estimate for developing the portal was based on a functional scope that did not include all of the mandatory features identified by the Data Portal Work Group. The current level of EN funding is insufficient to deliver a portal

---

[11] In July 2013, the SDWIS NextGen system was renamed to SDWIS Primacy Agency, or SDWIS Prime. The reason for the name change is to emphasize that this new system is specifically designed for the drinking water primacy agencies.

delivering the mandatory features.

**Tier 2 Activities:**

**Development of Web services** that consume SDWIS Prime data for use with external primacy agency business systems. Examples of external primacy agency business systems include systems used to manage water system engineering plan reviews, operator certifications, water system permitting and fee collection, and such.

**Modification of primacy agency external business systems** that interact with SDWIS Prime to replace ODBC and similar connections used with SDWIS State and other systems with Web service calls.

# Underground Injection Control (UIC) Database

**Description:**

EPA launched new a UIC national database in Dec 2007 and immediately began accepting data through EPA's Exchange Network. The UIC database is designed to provide high quality, consistent, and complete information to support EPA's objective to manage and oversee the national and regional delegated program. Data fields are at the well level, with fields for UIC inventory (linked to FRS), permits, geospatial coordinates, inspections, mechanical integrity, violations, and enforcement actions.

As of April 2014, 30 of the 69 state and regional UIC programs had successfully submitted data to the UIC database, including 15 primacy agencies that had fully transitioned to electronic reporting, and with an additional 19 programs submitting a one-time inventory dataset.

A revised XML document (Version 2.0) was released in 2010 under the same UIC data model to improve performance. After UIC programs complete mapping their data to the UIC Database XML schema they are expected to start submitting data twice annually between April 1, 2015 and July 1, 2015 and Oct 1, 2015 and November 15, 2015.

Each state is expected to transition from existing reporting to a biannual submission (reduced from quarterly) to the UIC database once it meets the data quality and completeness requirements.

| Exchange Network Program Office Activities | |
|---|---|
| **Milestone** | **Target Completion** |
| Release revised XML Schema – (Version 2.0) | Completed |
| Revised flow configuration document, other documentation completed | Completed |
| *Other:* Successful mapping, conversion of state data consistent with EPA mapping instructions, and node to node submission | 2015 |
| *Other:* Validation of data received in EPA's database after each biannual submission to address QA/QC data issues and to continue until transition to e-reporting, transition to e-reporting are met. | Ongoing |

**Additional Activities to be considered by Grant Applicants**

- EPA will support activities to build local data systems for Class V state programs with no effective existing database, to support efficient data transfer to EPA's database. EPA has existing data templates and data transfer tools available. *(Tier 2)*

- In order to transition to electronic reporting through the Exchange Network, EPA requests UIC applicants to address the resolution of QA/QC issues raised during biannual data submission cycles. *(Tier 2)*

*Note: These activities are eligible for funding provided that the proposal commits to putting the UIC data flow into production, transitions the data flow to the virtual node and places into production, and/or puts publishing/data availability applications or Web pages into production.*

# Water Quality
# Exchange (WQX)

## Description:

Water Quality eXchange (WQX) defines the framework by which EPA compiles water quality monitoring data (physical, chemical, biological, habitat, metrics, and index) into the STOrage and RETrieval (STORET) Data Warehouse (http://www.epa.gov/storet/dw_home.html). Data from multi-jurisdictional entities (including State and Tribal agencies) are shared with EPA via the WQX schema and made available from STORET at a national level via a seamless collection of monitoring data. For more information about WQX, please visit http://www.epa.gov/storet/wqx/index.html or http://www.exchangenetwork.net/exchanges/water/wqx.htm.

In addition, data from STORET can be queried using the EPA and USGS co-hosted Water Quality Portal http://waterqualitydata.us.

| Exchange Network Program Office Activities | |
|---|---|
| **Milestone** | **Target Completion Date** |
| System readiness to receive test and production data to EPA WQX v3.0. The new v3.0 will include minor field updates. (note WQX v1.0, 2.0, and 2.1 will still be accepted) | Spring 2015 |
| Develop biological web services to be served out of the Water Quality Portal | Summer 2014 |
| Develop habitat, metrics and index web services to be served out of the Water Quality Portal | Summer 2015 |

** The STORET Warehouse web mapping services are available at the following URL: http://www.epa.gov/waters/geoservices/docs/waters_mapping_services. html. Note that two separate services exist for STORET: STORET_NAD83 and STORET_WMERC.

## Additional Activities to be considered by Grant Applicants:

- Utilize the most recent version of the WQX schema to flow physical, chemical, biological, habitat, metric and index monitoring data. The new WQX v3.0 will include minor field updates. All earlier WQX versions (v1.0, v2.0, v2.1) will still be accepted. *(Tier 2)*
- Develop applications that use EPA STORET Warehouse or Water Quality Portal web services (data and spatial) for data integration and analysis (e.g., establish links to water impairment, water permit facilities, watershed resource planning). *(Tier 1)*
- Adopt and encourage all applicable data standards for data submission and

sharing. *(Tier 2)*

- Identify innovative ways for sharing monitoring data *(Tier 1)*, such as:
    o Expand within-state data partners flowing data (e.g. other agencies or watershed groups) including ambient monitoring, cyclic/periodic/event monitoring, surveys, and utilities/facilities
    o Encourage capacity with small data providers through WQX and WQX Web
    o Identify methods and approaches to share continuous monitoring data among Exchange Network community
    o Explore ways to make water data discoverable through development of publishing services (e.g. leveraging Virtual Node or Virtual Node related plans). *(Tier 1)*
- Encourage the development of common catalogue services that provide standard water quality data discovery and publishing to the Exchange Network community. *(Tier 2)*
- Build tools using Exchange Network application programming interfaces (API) technologies, services and specifications that integrate water quality data from various sources (*e.g.* Water Quality Portaldata) to present a common view of water quality data. *(Tier 1)*
- Begin linking station locations consistent with the NHD and the Geospatial One Stop Hydrography Standard. Implement NHDEvent data flow for STORET/WQX monitoring locations that have been geo-referenced to the NHD. *(Tier 2)*

*Eligible for funding as a Tier 2 priority (for partners implementing new flows or upgrading existing flows), provided that the project proposal commits to deploying the new (or upgraded) flow into production.*

## Assessment TMDL Tracking & ImplementatioN System (ATTAINS) (Integrated Reporting (303(d)/305(b))

**Description:**

The Assessment TMDL Tracking And Implementation System (ATTAINS) includes state-reported information, required under Clean Water Act (CWA) Sections 303(d) and 305(b), regarding state assessment of the support of designated uses in assessed waters, identified causes and sources of impairment, identified impaired waters including their location, and Total Maximum Daily Load (TMDL) status. EPA and the states invest a significant amount of resources in meeting these requirements using a combination of paper and electronic submissions. In the most recent ICR for the 303(d)/305(b) program, it is estimated that the state burden alone is $193 million a year.

ATTAINS allows EPA to streamline and improve the Report to Congress required under CWA Section 305(b) by providing electronic access to the national and state summaries and the detailed waterbody-specific assessment status reported by states. Under EPA's new Water Quality Framework[12], one activity being pursued is a redesign of ATTAINS. This redesign will replace both the distributed Assessment Database (ADB) and the current OWIR-ATT flow. The new ATTAINS will be a cloud-based application that states, tribes[13], and EPA can use to track water quality assessment decisions, TMDLs, priority areas, and report on strategic measures. A goal of this redesign is to move the Integrated Reporting process to a paperless process as envisioned by EPA's E-Enterprise initiative, and it is envisioned that the Exchange Network will play a key role in managing the workflow from state/tribal-submitted data to EPA for review and approval. This redesign will include a new Exchange Network ATTAINS data flow that will both allow for the two-way exchange of data between states and EPA, and will also allow for the publishing of IR data via web services that will support the integrated vision of the Water Quality Framework. The new ATTAINS data flow will include the ability for states/tribes to provide water quality assessment information (including use support, causes, and sources), provide and receive TMDL information, provide references to water quality monitoring location data that are relevant to the water quality assessments (and submitted via the Water Quality Exchange [WQX]), provide identification of state priorities, and provide activities that states are performing that lead to water quality restoration.

The ATTAINS redesign will be completed in two phases: the first phase will be complete in early FY 2016, and the second phase will be complete in FY 2017. EPA is working with states to define the requirements for this new system, and is also developing a draft data model and schema. EPA is looking for state and tribal partners to evaluate the new ATTAINS data

---

[12] **The Water Quality Framework (Framework)** is a new way of thinking about how EPA's water quality data and information systems can be better integrated to more effectively support water quality managers and meet program goals. The Framework will streamline water quality assessment and reporting currently performed under ATTAINS, eliminate paper reporting and provide a more complete picture of the nation's water quality. The Framework will start by focusing on better integrating three systems: 1) EPA's water quality monitoring repository (STORET and the Water Quality Exchange [WQX]), 2) EPA's Assessment TMDL Tracking and ImplementatioN System (ATTAINS), and 3) EPA's surface water mapping tool (the National Hydrography Dataset Plus [NHDPlus]). Following the integration of these systems, further integration is possible with other water programs such as: water quality permits, enforcement and compliance, source water protection, and nonpoint source projects.

[13] Tribes can provide water quality assessments as part of their 305(b) reports. Tribes would be able to use this new ATTAINS system for tracking and reporting this information.

flow for the 2016 Integrated Reporting Cycle. States should also plan to transition to the new ATTAINS by the 2018 Integrated Reporting Cycle. In order to make this transition, states can either use the new Exchange Network ATTAINS data flow, or be direct users of the new cloud-based ATTAINS data system (or some combination of the two). The OWIR-ATT data flow will no longer be supported starting with the 2018 Integrated Reporting Cycle.

Because of the changes that will result from the ATTAINS redesign, for the purposes of the Exchange Network Grant program, the new ATTAINS data flow is considered a new flow, and not an enhancement to the existing OWIR-ATT data flow. States currently using the OWIR-ATT data flow are eligible for receiving grants to provide data via the new ATTAINS data flow.

EPA recommends that states do not pursue developing a OWIR-ATT data flow for the 2016 Integrated Reporting cycle or beyond.

| Exchange Network Program Office Activities | |
|---|---|
| Milestone | Target Completion Date |
| ATTAINS v1.0[14] draft schema available for review and input | Fall 2014 |
| ATTAINS v1.0 draft Flow Configuration Document available for review and input | Fall 2014 |
| Launch Integrated Project Team (IPT) to evaluate system dataflow and data elements (outreach) | Winter 2014 |
| Final ATTAINS v1.0 schema and Flow Configuration Document | Spring 2015 |
| States pilot ATTAINS v1.0 flow for the 2016 Integrated Reporting Cycle | Spring 2016 |
| Compile lessons learned from 2016 Integrated Reporting Cycle | Summer-Winter 2016 |
| Compile updates for ATTAINS v1.0 schema and Flow Configuration Document | Winter 2016 |
| Draft ATTAINS v1.1 schema and Flow Configuration Document | Winter 2016 |
| Final ATTAINS v1.1 schema and Flow Configuration Document | Spring 2017 |
| End support for OWIR-ATT data flow and schema | Summer 2017 |
| Full transition to new ATTAINS Flow for the 2018 Integrated Reporting Cycle | Spring 2018 |

[14] As described in the text, the ATTAINS v1.0 schema is replacing the OWIR-ATT schema. EPA recommends that states do not pursue developing OWIR-ATT data flows for the 2016 Integrated Reporting cycle or beyond.

**Additional Activities to be considered by Grant Applicants:**

- Participate in the new ATTAINS data flow pilot in preparation for the 2016 Integrated Reporting Cycle, including submitting data via the new ATTAINS data flow. For the 2016 Integrated Reporting Cycle, EPA will accept data in either the new ATTAINS v1.0 schema or the OWIR-ATT schema, but will only accept data in the ATTAINS schema for the 2018 Integrated Reporting Cycle and beyond.

- Identify innovative tools that may enhance the interaction between EPA Regions and states during the 303(d)/IR review and approval process.

- Identify innovative ways to share geospatial information related to Integrated Reporting data and utilize Web-based services and applications.

- Identify innovative ways to integrate water quality monitoring and assessment information, including developing innovative, reusable tools that make use of web services to both discover and make use of water quality monitoring data in a more automated way.

*Note:* *All activities are eligible for funding as* **Tier 1** *priorities provided that the project proposal commits to deploying the ATTAINS dataflow into production.*

**Facility Registry System
(FRS)**

**Description:**

The Facility Registry System (FRS) is EPA's centrally managed database that integrates facility data across nearly 90 EPA and other federal systems, as well as numerous state, tribal and territorial databases, which provides access to the names, locations, associated program IDs, industrial classification, corporate and contact affiliation, and other information for facilities subject to environmental regulations and for other sites of environmental interest. These integrated facility identification records allow EPA, its state and tribal partners, Web application owners, and the public to access integrated environmental information reported from and about facilities and sites. The Facility Id 3.0 (FACID 3.0) schema is now available and allows EN partners to publish and access facility identification information more easily. FACID 2.3 is still available and supported for those partners not yet ready to move to FACID 3.0.

Applicants that wish to take advantage of FRS Web services can find a listing of data resources here: http://www.epa.gov/enviro/html/fii/dataresources.html and should periodically check RCS (see Appendix K for a description), a catalog of IT resources from EPA and its state and tribal partners. Resources will be added to this location on a regular basis.

**Additional Activities to be considered by Grant Applicants:**

- Collaborative efforts among tribes to use the Facility Linkage Application (FLA) to reconcile, correct and analyze data and assess data quality prior to projects requiring the sharing of facility information. *(Tier 2)*
- Encourage state and tribal programs to use the FRS Lookup service in order to integrate data by FRS ID. *(Tier 2)*
    - This activity can also include integrating other state/tribe/territory programs in order to incorporate additional environmental interests (e.g., air, water, waste, etc.) for partner use.
    - Partners that integrate their facility information can use this service to develop tools for retrieving additional value-added data fields into their facility records, including geocoded addresses, NAICS codes, applicable census information, hydrologic unit codes (HUC), and congressional boundary information.
    - Partners that integrate their facility information can also use this service to develop tools for retrieving FRS data for comparative analysis and reconciliation.
- Collaborative projects between EPA and partners on pilot projects that develop mobile platforms or device agnostic services which leverage FRS APIs for field data collection, review and correction of locations, subfacility features and facility details. Funds can be used to support intergovernmental IPTs for scoping state inspection tools or other mobile solutions which leverage FRS resources and support transactions with

regulated entities. *(Tier 1)*

- Burden reduction efforts that utilize comparative analysis and crosswalking of data elements across programs relative to state/federal statutes and regulations and relevant standards, identifying where data elements of a state diverge with those of FRS, and where they can be harmonized or managed via shared taxonomies *(Tier 1)*
- Use of the FRS Lookup service for front end data entry for the purposes of burden reduction as well as supporting entry of data integrated by FRS ID. *(Tier 1)*
  - o This activity can also include integrating other state/tribe/territory programs in order to incorporate additional environmental interests (e.g., air, water, waste, etc.) for partner use.
  - o Partners that integrate their facility information can use this service to develop tools for retrieving additional value-added data fields into their facility records, including geocoded addresses, NAICS codes, applicable census information, hydrologic unit codes (HUC), and congressional boundary information.
  - o Partners that integrate their facility information can also use this service to develop tools for retrieving FRS data for comparative analysis and reconciliation.

## Substance Registry Services (SRS)

**Description:**

The Substance Registry Services (SRS) is a shared service that:
1. Enables data integration by chemical;
2. Increases data quality of chemical names and other identifiers in systems and online forms;
3. Promotes information management by EPA programs, states, and tribes of chemical lists;
4. Helps the public and other users discover which systems and programs have data and under which chemical name.

SRS is USEPA's centralized resource for basic information about chemicals, biological organisms, and other substances that are tracked or regulated by EPA or other organizations (e.g., state agencies, tribal agencies, other federal agencies). It is a window that helps the public discover which EPA program or partner may have data for a substance.

There is a record for each substance; each record contains basic information about the substance, such as Chemical Abstract Service (CAS) Name and CAS number. Importantly, SRS includes synonyms, which can help the public or other users discover substances of interest. There are also links to health and safety fact sheets developed internally at EPA or externally by states, other federal agencies, or international organizations. In addition, SRS catalogs substances into programmatic and statutory lists, showing which substances are on which list and the synonyms used by each list.

There are several services available for use by partner systems. To promote information management of chemical identification, SRS can register state and tribal programmatic lists. States and tribes also can improve public access to health and safety information by creating direct links from their websites to individual SRS records. SRS also has a widget that states and tribes can incorporate into their web pages.

Web services are available for partners to pull information from SRS directly into their system to be used to improve data quality for online reporting forms or other tools. The Toxics Release Inventory and the Chemical Data Reporting (CDR) are two examples of programs that have incorporated SRS web services into their online reports. When entering chemical names on the reports, a facility searches for a chemical using a synonym or other identifier. The facility then selects the appropriate chemical, which was pulled from SRS. This online reporting saved the CDR program hundreds of thousands of dollars in reduced data quality errors.

**Additional Activities to be considered by Grant Applicants:**
- Work with the SRS team to add state or tribal lists to SRS to make it possible to cross-walk chemicals, regardless of synonym, between states, tribes, and EPA. (**Tier 2**)
- Add SRS Identifiers to state or tribal systems to promote the ability to link across datasets by substance, regardless of which synonyms are used. (**Tier 2**)

A-33

- Encourage state or tribal programs to integrate SRS web services into online reporting forms or other tools to improve the data quality of substance identities or to help submitters report for the correct substance. (**Tier 1**)
- Collaborative projects between EPA and partners on pilot projects that develop mobile platforms or device agnostic services which leverage SRS APIs during field data collection, review and correction of substance identities. Funds can be used to support intergovernmental IPTs for scoping state inspection tools or other mobile solutions which leverage SRS resources and support transactions with regulated entities. (**Tier 1**)

SRS can be access at www.epa.gov/srs

For further questions, please contact John Harman in US EPA's Office of Environmental Information (OEI) at: 202 566 0748; or by email at: harman.john@epa.gov

# Toxics Release Inventory System
# (TRIS)

## Description:

The TRI System is an annual reporting requirement for industries with toxic chemical releases (deadline is July 1st of every year). The TRI Data Exchange (TDX) provides for simultaneous submission of TRI reports to both EPA and states via CDX. Benefits of the TRI Data Exchange include:

- For participating states and EPA, elimination of duplicative data entry, reduction of state data reconciliation, and faster access to the data
- For facilities, reduced burden through simultaneous submission to both EPA and the state to meet EPCRA Section 313 reporting requirements

| Exchange Network Program Office Activities | |
|---|---|
| **Milestones** | **Target Completion Date** |
| Load/Update XML Schema (if necessary) for FY 2014 | 11/30/2014 |
| Continue to investigate use of additional Web services for further application functionality | Ongoing |
| Test and Support operational Node-to-Node data exchanges between | Ongoing |

## Additional Activities to be considered by Grant Applicants:

Work with the TRI Program to test XML schema on the state node to accept TRI data from EPA.

- States should develop procedures that enable the import of TRI data into their systems. The procedures should support data in XML format received via their state node.
- Encourage environmental state program office employees at TDX states to take advantage of the benefits offered by the TDX Viewer tool. More information about the TDX Viewer can be accessed at http://www2.epa.gov/toxics-release-inventory-tri-program/tdx-viewer-information
- Use the TRI XML schema to develop loading/converter tools to populate the state database directly from incoming data sources via CDX.
- Leverage existing tools and services developed by states already on the TRI Data Exchange. A map displaying current TDX participants can be accessed at http://www2.epa.gov/toxics-release-inventory-tri-program/tri-data-exchange
- Collaborate with states on the TRI Data Exchange and other states interested in joining (i.e., participate in monthly TDX conference calls, develop sharable code)

  _Note:_ _These activities are eligible for funding as **Tier 2** priorities provided that the project proposal commits to deploying the outbound dataflow into production_

## Enabling Geospatial Data Exchange

**Description:**

Geospatial data represent features on Earth expressed as points, lines, or polygons and are used in tandem with programmatic data, through geospatial information systems and browsers, to support programmatic analysis using a geographic or place-based context.

Office of Management and Budget (OMB) Circular A-16 "Coordination of Geographic Information and Related Spatial Data Activities" identifies 16 critical geospatial data themes that are essential components of the National Spatial data infrastructure (NSDI) (http://www.whitehouse.gov/omb/circulars/a016/a016_rev.html). The A-16 geospatial data theme categories encompass a wide variety of place-based data sets which are essential to environmental analysis and decision-making. These include, but are not limited to data related to biodiversity, geology, cultural resources, administrative units and boundaries, parcels and cadastre, wetlands, watershed boundaries, soils, hydrography, imagery, transportation, and elevation.

- The Exchange Network can be particularly useful for publishing geospatial data when any of the following conditions apply:
- data needs to flow securely
- large payloads of data, requiring automated machine-to-machine delivery
- data needs to be delivered to multiple locations simultaneously (such as inspections, enforcement, or facilities data collected in the field that ends in a flow to one or more state programs, an EPA program office, and the Facility Registry Service)
- the data is already accessible through a node
- the data are needed immediately for disaster and emergency response
- data is used to update and maintain large national datasets (see activity below)

**Additional Activities to be considered by Grant Applicants:**
- **Emergency Response and Recovery Data Flows**: Development and rapid deployment (anywhere, anytime) of secure geospatial Web services (e.g., Web feature services), on the EN virtual node, to support joint State, local and/or Federal response and recovery activities. Priority is given to data flows and schema for the critical information requirements to emergency incidents that may involve significant environmental impacts. Critical information includes accurate geographic coordinates; current facility names, contact personnel and their phone numbers; and rapid assessment or operational status for drinking water and wastewater treatment plants, facilities subject to RMP (Remedial Project Manager) and/or FRP (Facility Response Plan) requirements and facilities subject to SARA 311/312 Tier 1 reporting requirements. Additionally, current geospatial data and operational status for an area's utility infrastructure (e.g., electrical, gas, water, phone, etc.) and the areas current local cadastral data (tax parcels with ownership). Grantees should engage State, local and Federal responders, such as, EPA Data Team; to help plan, develop, test and consume these Web services. **(Tier 1)**

- **Advanced Facility Monitoring and Enforcement:** A comparison of continuous monitoring data and/or advanced emissions monitoring data (for criteria or air toxics pollutants) to permit data and/or human health risk thresholds. The project will include GIS visualization and will indicate where monitoring exceeds permit limits or risk thresholds. The information can be used to identify potential targets for compliance evaluations and to identify trends in source categories and industry sectors for Exchange Network partners. **(Tier 1\*)**

- Collaborative pilot projects between EPA and partners on pilot projects that develop mobile platforms or device agnostic services which leverage EPA APIs for field data collection, review and correction of locations, subfacility features and facility details. *(Tier 1)*

*\*This activity is eligible for funding as a Tier 1 priority if the project proposal commits to deploying into production an application or publishing service that utilizes this capability.*

## Cloud Transition Grants for EN Partners

The Exchange Network Grant Program encourages projects that promote efficiency through the reuse of shared systems and resources. The Exchange Network governance established an integrated project team (IPT) consisting of states, tribes and EPA to review the feasibility of and to develop requirements for a cloud-based node. The IPT developed the Virtual Node Guidance and Recommendations Document v1.0 (http://www.exchangenetwork.net/virtual-node-ipt/ ), which was used by EPA to create a virtual node in the cloud. This virtual node was designed to help partners - particularly small and medium-sized organizations - find even more cost efficient ways to manage their nodes and decrease development and operational costs. Using this shared cloud node platform helps partners eliminate the need for maintaining node servers and software locally.

The Virtual Node, which is analogous to a central shared node platform, can be individually configured by each partner to handle its different dataflows. EPA has established the Virtual Node infrastructure in a central shared cloud environment. This new node model was developed in response to Exchange Network partners that need more cost efficient ways to manage their nodes and decrease costs. This new approach has potential to significantly simplify development and maintenance of both nodes and flows using inheritance features and plug-in support. The specific design details of this model are being tested by EPA and early adopters in coordination with the Network Technology Board.

The focus of this solicitation is to cover the transition cost for partners to move from a physical node implementation to the virtual node multi-tenant (shared) implementation. Funding for Virtual Node adoption will not exceed $70,000. Actual award amounts will be based upon the complexity of moving individual nodes and associated dataflows (e.g., number of active dataflows) to this environment.

**Virtual Node Application**

EPA is interested in working closely with partners to leverage this new model for a shared node Implementation (partners sharing a common scalable node). Installations of this type would provide a simplified solution for any partner (particularly partners lacking adequate resources for a dedicated node environment). Much of the basic administration would be done centrally, so that partners are able to concentrate on configuring data flows and publishing new services and data instead of administering node application servers.

Under the Virtual Node solution:

- Partners would configure data flows on the new centrally-hosted virtual cloud node, but partner databases could stay in place.
- State databases would connect to the Virtual Node through a new secure

channel or backend bridge.

- Node administrators would retain complete control of all aspects of their Node, their data flows, and the manner in which the virtual node accesses their staging tables or databases.
- Wizard-driven functionality is available on the virtual node for creating new data flows and to minimize the effort to create and transition data flows to the virtual node.

The virtual node may offer some significant advantages over current nodes. It eliminates software licensing costs, server costs, and much of the administration costs for partners, while providing a simplified development model and greater economies of scale.

Applications for transitioning to the virtual node should focus on development activities such as:
    a) Dataflow configuration,
    b) Testing,
    c) Security Plan Requirements, and
    d) Virtual Node Training.

**New Node Communication Model**

Another key goal of the solicitation is to explore various ways of interconnecting from the partner staging tables or database servers (backend) to the virtual node in the cloud environment. The following technical options are currently available:

- Internet Service Bus (ISB): A component will be installed in the partner backend database environment which establishes an SSL tunnel with the ISB in the cloud for relaying network activity to/from the node in the cloud. The component is supplied by CDX and installed as a Windows NT service. No firewall change is required.
- Secure Virtual Private Network (VPN): This is a secure network connection from the partner's node in the cloud to the partner backend database environment. Once the connectivity is established, the node can make direct database connections through the secure channel. This is the traditional VPN approach and the partner must open a firewall for VPN access.

Partners are encouraged to evaluate one or more of these options with their security team to ensure that a communication model can be approved for their virtual node implementation. Partners should include their target models in their grant.

# Appendix C

## Shared CROMERR Services

### Background

EPA's Cross Media Electronic Reporting Regulation (CROMERR) sets technology-neutral and performance based standards for systems used by states, tribes and local governments to receive electronic reports and documents from entities regulated under EPA-authorized programs. These standards cover a variety of system functions (e.g., security, user identification, etc.) designed to make electronic reports as legally defensible as paper submittals.

To date, states and local governments have typically addressed CROMERR requirements by implementing system functions within their respective electronic reporting systems resulting in some duplicative investment of resources. Budget shortfalls, staff turnover, changing technology and complex program requirements pose challenges to organizations required to implement CROMERR and continue this duplicative investment.

In an effort to ease these challenges, the Exchange Network Leadership Council established the Shared CROMERR Services Integrated Project Team (IPT), comprised of EPA management and staff and 17 state representatives, in the Fall of 2012. The IPT discussed and investigated opportunities for the adoption of information technology services that EPA maintains and co-regulators could use to meet CROMERR requirements. This Executive Summary broadly reviews the recommendations from the IPT and the actions that EPA is taking to assist our trading partners.

### Description of Shared CROMERR Services

EPA is offering CROMERR services that can be reused and managed in a centralized way, and co-regulators can leverage the CDX CROMERR services for their own reporting programs in a more cost effective and efficient manner. EPA will offer states and tribes a set of CDX services for CROMERR functions; states and tribes will be able to select the desired services and implement them to meet their organizational and system needs.

At a summary level, the services can be broken down into the following three categories:
- **Registration and Identity Management:**
  - Services for creating, validating and maintaining accounts of reporting entities.
  - Over 90 percent of IPT participants are interested in implementing a shared solution to help with Identity Proofing components within the Registration process.

- **Electronic Signature:**
    - Services for authenticating credentials, verifying user intent, and electronically signing submissions from regulated entities that is as legally defensible as the traditional pen and paper approach.
    - Over 80 percent of the IPT participants are interested in implementing a shared solution to help with the signature ceremony aspects of CROMERR.
- **Copy of Record (COR) Management:**
    - Services for storing, maintaining, and retrieving data submissions at the level of legal integrity required by CROMERR.
    - Nearly 70 percent of IPT participants are interested in implementing a shared solution that would help with COR management.

## Anticipated Benefits

The following benefits are anticipated as a result of providing Shared CROMERR Services to states and tribes:

- **Reduced barriers for compliance** – The initial upfront and ongoing investment to meet CROMERR requirements will be reduced.
- **Improved CROMERR Compliance Assistance** – Adoption of Shared CROMERR Services will facilitate better responses to CROMERR compliance auditing activities.
- **Realization of Cost Savings** – There is great potential for states and tribes will realize costs savings by integrating shared CROMERR services as opposed to building, operating and maintaining independent systems.
- **Common Support Model** – States and tribes will be able to leverage a common pool of resources, services and lessons learned to assist with implementation approaches and integration work.
- **User Friendly Experience to Regulated Communities** – States and tribes will be able to provide consistent and simplified registration and electronic signature processes to the regulated community.
- **Consistent Audit and Enforcement Practices** – Shared CROMERR services should provide a stronger legal foundation and more consistent practices in civil and criminal enforcement proceedings.

## Current Status

EPA has implemented a set of CROMERR shared services and is working with EN partners to test and use them. Numerous states have established plans for implementing the necessary business processes and technical environments to consume these services. EPA is conducting a series of continual improvement sessions to get feedback on service refinements and explore opportunities for expansion of the services. The CROMERR Shared Services IPT is continuing as a mechanism to educate new EN partners and make future implementation easier. More Information is available on the IPT and status of the services at the EN website: http://www.exchangenetwork.net/shared-cromerr-services-ipt/

## Exchange Network Grant Opportunities

Exchange Network Partners with a need to implement CROMERR for their electronic reporting programs can choose to leverage EPA's centralized CROMERR services with support from the Grant Program. Acceptable activities include but are not limited to the following:

- Integrating CROMERR services into exchange partner dataflows,
- Documenting technical and security requirements,
- Testing and deploying CROMERR services,
- Participating on and supporting the State/EPA CROMERR IPT(s), and
- Project planning and management.

# Appendix D

## Detailed Instructions for Submitting Applications

Applicants for the FY 2015 Exchange Network Grant program must submit an application package to EPA by November 24, 2014. EPA will accept applications for National Environmental Information Exchange Network grants in one of two ways: 1) an application submitted electronically through the grants.gov website; or 2) a hardcopy mailed or delivered application, including one original and two copies. Applicants who submit a hard copy are encouraged to also submit an electronic courtesy copy of the application by email, to Salena Reynolds at ENGrantProgram@epa.gov. EPA will confirm receipt of each application with an e-mail to the contacts listed in the cover letter. **A single proposal can be for either Exchange Network or E-Enterprise-related categories, but not for both.**

EPA will notify applicants of its selection decisions in or around April 2015. The notification letters will include further instructions to successful applicants for submittal of additional or updated documents. EPA plans to award all grants by July 31, 2015.

**The following forms and documents are required under this announcement** (fillable forms can be obtained from http://www.epa.gov/ogd/forms/forms.htm):

1. Application for Federal Assistance (SF-424)
2. Budget Information for Non-Construction Programs (SF-424A)
3. Assurances for Non-Construction Programs (SF-424B)
4. Certification Regarding Lobbying Form
5. EPA Key Contacts Form 5700-54
6. EPA Form 4700-4 – Preaward Compliance Review Report
7. Project Narrative
8. Detailed Itemized Budget
9. Disclosure of Lobbying Activities (SF-LLL), if applicable
10. Negotiated Indirect Cost Rate Agreement, if applicable
11. Programmatic Resources and Personnel
12. Cover Letter
13. Additional Information for Inter-tribal Consortium, if applicable
14. Formal Project Partners Roles and Responsibilities, if applicable
15. List of Federally and/or Non-federally Funded Assistance Agreements

### 1. Standard Form (SF) 424, Application for Federal Assistance
Complete the form. Please note that the organizational Dun and Bradstreet (D&B) Data Universal Number System (DUNS) number must be included on the SF-424. Organizations may obtain a DUNS number at no cost by calling the toll-free DUNS number request line at 1-866- 705-5711.

**2. SF-424A, Budget Information for Non-Construction Programs**
Complete the form. The total amount of federal funding requested for the project period should be shown on line 5(e) and on line 6(k) of SF-424A. If indirect costs are included, the amount of indirect costs should be entered on line 6(j). The indirect cost rate (i.e., a percentage), the base (e.g., personnel costs and fringe benefits), and the amount should also be indicated on line 22. If indirect costs are requested, a copy of the Negotiated Indirect Cost Rate Agreement must be submitted as part of the application package. (See instructions for document 10 below.)

**3. SF-424B, Assurances for Non-Construction Program**
Complete the form.

**4. EPA Lobbying Form – Certification Regarding Lobbying**
Complete the form.

**5. EPA Form 5700-54, Key Contacts Form**
Complete the form.

**6. EPA Form 4700-4, Pre-Award Compliance Review Report.**
Complete the form.

**7. Project Narrative**

1. **General Guidelines for Writing a Successful Project Narrative**
   a. **Clarity and Succinctness** - A proposed work plan must not exceed ten pages. Any work plan elements that appear after the tenth page are not reviewed. Grant panels score proposals on how well they meet the criteria. The narrative should completely describe how the proposal meets each criterion.
   b. **Completeness and continuity** – Make sure the project narrative fully addresses each criterion. Make sure all items that belong in the work plan are grouped together and that no non-work plan items are included in this portion of the application.
   c. **Numbering**– Number each page of your work plan from one to ten.
   d. **Legibility** – Proposals should use fonts (serif or sans serif) that are 11 point or higher. Use 1-inch margins and single line spacing. Small font size across full pages is not necessary (see 1.a) and it makes a reviewer's job harder.
   e. **Limit the Terminology to "Goals, Outputs and Outcomes."** There are no "objectives, milestones, or tasks" in Exchange Network Grant proposals. There is nothing wrong with those terms. In fact, you might find them useful for your internal project planning and tracking. However, limiting and standardizing these terms makes it easier for panelists to score proposals consistently.
2. **Work Plan Contents** – Include each of the following items in the ten-page project narrative.
   a. **General Introduction** – This should be a narrative description of the proposed work. If the proposal is for more than one project, it may be helpful to organize the introduction by goal. An introduction is not an evaluation criterion but it will help reviewers better understand what is being proposed.

b. **Describe project goals, outputs and outcomes that lead to environmental results** - Include a plan that allows the applicant to track and report progress toward achieving the project's proposed goals. Reviewers will look for a table similar to the one included below as evidence of a plan to track and report progress. Using the table below as a model will ensure reviewers can see what major project outputs (major deliverables or events) you propose for each goal (a self-contained project), when they are scheduled and what overall outcomes leading to environmental results each proposed goal supports.

**Goals, Outputs, Scheduled Completion Dates and Outcomes**
*Suggested format – expand number of goal and outputs as needed*

| Goal | Output | Scheduled Completion Date | Outcome(s) |
|---|---|---|---|
| Goal 1: Name the Goal | 1.1 | | |
| | 1.2 | | |
| | 1.3 | | |
| | 1.4 | | |
| Goal 2: Name the Goal | 2.1 | | |
| | 2.2 | | |
| | 2.3 | | |

c. **Roles and responsibilities of project participants for the applicant and any partners** - If the project is not a partnership, list who is going to work on the project and what they will be doing. If the proposed project includes one or more formal partners, describe what their roles as agencies or tribes are.

d. **Programmatic involvement in the development and management of the project, including a listing of programmatic participants, positions and roles in the project** –Any project that is not purely technical must have substantive program participation. Make sure that you describe that contribution.

e. **(EN applications only) Applicant's commitment to re-use existing EN tools by searching for existing resources, to share new tools with EN partners or registering any newly developed resources in The Exchange Network Discovery Service (ENDS) or Reusable Component Services (RCS) as appropriate** – Applicants should not spend grant funds on tools already developed and available for EN partner use. The proposal must include a commitment to use or adapt existing tools. Applicants must also commit to registering tools they develop in grant funded projects.

f.  **(EE applications only) Applicant's commitment to adopt a methodology and develop products are applicable to EPA and its co-implementer partners nationally.**

g.  **Budget amounts for each goal** – For proposals with more than one goal, list the total budget amount allocated to each. Occasionally EPA will decide an individual goal should not be funded. This may happen when a proposed goal is not consistent with EN priorities or when EPA decides the proposal is not adequate for other reasons. Because each goal represents a free-standing project, EPA may decide to fund other proposed goals in the same proposal. Knowing what each proposed project will cost makes it possible for EPA to adjust the total budget in these cases.

h.  **Summarized qualifications of the project manager and other key personnel**

i.  **Statement summarizing past performance**

## 8. Detailed Itemized Budget

Applicants should describe **both the total project budget and the costs associated with each major goal** in a detailed itemized budget. *The goal-specific budget information is important, because EPA may wish to consider partially funding some projects (i.e., funding only some goals for a project but not others). Failure to provide a detailed itemized budget will result in a mandatory 10-point deduction on your application.* The budget must include any relevant item listed below:

A.  Personnel – List all staff positions by title. Give the annual salary of each person, the percentage of their time devoted to the project, the amount of each person's salary funded by the grant and the total personnel cost for the budget period.

B.  Fringe Benefits – Identify the fringe benefit rate and total amount.

C.  Travel – Specify the mileage, per diem, estimated number of in state and out of state trips other costs for each type of travel. EPA suggests that applicants include funds for travel to national, regional and area Exchange Network conferences.

D.  Equipment – Identify each item of equipment to be purchased that has an estimated acquisition cost of $5,000 or more per unit and a useful lifetime of more than one year. List the quantity and unit cost per item. Items with a unit cost of less than $5,000 are supplies.

E. Supplies – Supplies include all tangible personal property other than "equipment." The detailed budget should identify categories of supplies (such as laboratory supplies or office supplies). List the quantity and unit cost per item.

F. Contractual – Identify each proposed contract and specify its purpose and estimated cost. Applicants who request in-kind services should list them here.

G. Other – List each item in sufficient detail for U.S. EPA to determine whether the costs are reasonable or allowable. List any item, such as training, not covered elsewhere here. This is also where Subawards should be allocated. Recognize that there is a difference between a procurement (goods and services) and a subaward (performing part of the project).

H. Indirect Charges – If indirect charges are included in the budget, include the approved indirect cost rate with a copy of the Indirect Cost Rate Agreement, a description of the base used to calculate indirect costs and total cost of the base, and the total indirect charges requested. **Before an applicant can incur any costs under the indirect cost category, the Indirect Cost Rate Agreement must be approved and current.** If you do not have a current rate, you may submit a copy of the submitted application to the cognizant fiduciary agency.

I. Management Fees – When formulating budgets for applications, applicants must not include management fees or similar charges in excess of the direct costs and indirect costs at the rate approved by the applicants cognizant audit agency, or at the rate provided for by the terms of the agreement negotiated with EPA. The term "management fees or similar charges" refers to expenses added to the direct costs in order to accumulate and reserve funds for ongoing business expenses, unforeseen liabilities, or for other similar costs that are not allowable under EPA assistance agreements. Management fees or similar charges may not be used to improve or expand the project funded under this agreement, except to the extent authorized as a direct cost of carrying out the scope of work.

J. Light Food Refreshments- If any light and/or refreshments are planning to be purchased with federal funds or matching funds, then a separate itemized breakout must be provided to determine whether or not the cost is considered reasonable and necessary.

## 9. SF-LLL, Disclosure of Lobbying Activities, if applicable
This form is required if your organization is involved in lobbying. Complete the form if your organization is involved in lobbying activities. Applicants that do not have to submit this form should state so in their application.

## 10. Negotiated Indirect Cost Rate Agreement

This form is required if indirect costs are included in the project budget. You must submit a copy of your organization's Indirect Cost Rate Agreement as part of the application package if your proposed budget includes indirect costs.

## 11. Programmatic Resources and Personnel:

Briefly describe the programmatic resources and personnel involved in the project for the recipient and any participating partner. Highlight any expertise or past experiences that may be particularly helpful in carrying out the project. Include biographical sketches or resumes of the lead and any partner Project Manager(s). Each biographical sketch should outline the education, work history, and knowledge/expertise of the individual that will be managing the proposed project. **(For proposals seeking funding for tribal capacity building who propose to use funding from this grant to hire key personnel and/or the project manager only -- submit a statement of knowledge, skills, abilities, and qualifications from the recruitment package for that position.)**

## 12. Cover Letter

Applications must include a cover letter signed by an authorized organizational representative (AOR) who, by virtue of their position, is able to obligate staff time on the proposed project (a suggested cover letter template is available at the end of Appendix E) including:
   i.   recipient information;
   ii.  project title;
   iii. **indication of whether the proposal is for a traditional Phase 2 (or Phase 1) Exchange Network or E-Enterprise related category.**
   iv.  type of vehicle requested (grant/cooperative agreement/ Performance Partnership Grant);
   v.   proposed amount of grant (broken down into direct funding and in-kind assistance if relevant);
   vi.  partners on the grant (if applicable);
   vii. brief project summary including a statement of project goal(s);
   viii. contact information for the project lead; and
   ix.  signature of executive level Authorized Organizational Representative (AOR).

## 13. Additional Information for Inter-tribal Consortium: 

An inter-tribal consortium applying for an FY 2015 Exchange Network Grant must include documentation that shows:
- a formal partnership exists among the Indian tribal governments that are members of the inter-tribal consortium, and the majority of the members are federally recognized Indian tribes; and,
- the consortium's federally recognized tribal members have authorized the consortium to apply for and receive assistance from the Exchange Network Grant Program.

## 14. Formal Project Partners – Roles and Responsibilities and Distribution of Funds:

If the proposed project involves formal project partners who will actively participate in implementing the project, provide a description of the roles and responsibilities of each partner in carrying out each of the project goals. Describe how the recipient would coordinate work among the partners using methods such as regular teleconferences, meetings, or written status reports. If the recipient plans to distribute funding to other partners, describe the method for doing so. Exchange Network grant projects that include one or more formal partners can have budgets up to $500,000.

Partnerships formed from within a single state, territorial or tribal government (e.g., a "partnership" limited to the Environment and Public Health Departments within a state) are not eligible partnerships and are limited to the $300,000 maximum funding for a single-jurisdiction grant and are not eligible for EE assistance agreements.

### 15. List of EN Assistance Agreements
Provide a list of previously awarded assistance agreements from the past three years.

## Submitting a Hard-Copy Application Package

Applicants should submit one original and two paper copies of all of the documents listed above (EPA has provided a checklist of required application documents in Appendix H). Hard-copy applications must be postmarked or delivered to an overnight mail or courier service at or before 11:59 PM (Eastern Standard Time) on November 24, 2014. *EPA recommends the use of overnight delivery or courier services to reduce the chance of delays.* Applicants should send their hard-copy applications to one of the following addresses depending on the delivery method:

**Mailing Address:**
Salena Reynolds
U.S. Environmental Protection Agency
1200 Pennsylvania Avenue, NW, (2823-T)
NW Washington, DC 20460

**Physical Address** *(for overnight, or courier deliveries)*:
Salena Reynolds
U.S. Environmental Protection Agency
1301 Constitution Avenue,
6th Floor, Room 6416S
Washington, DC 20004

Applicants who submit a hard copy are encouraged to also submit an electronic copy of the application by email, to Salena Reynolds at ENGrantProgram@epa.gov.

EPA will provide electronic acknowledgement of receipt of each application. If you do not receive acknowledgement of receipt from EPA regarding the submission of your grant application within 30 days of the application deadline, please contact Salena Reynolds, Exchange Network Grants Manager, at (202)-566-0466 or reynolds.salena@epa.gov. Failure to do so may result in your application not being considered. Please retain documentation that shows that you submitted your application by the deadline.

## Submitting an Electronic Application Package through Grants.gov

Electronic application packages can also be submitted through the grants.gov website, http://www.grants.gov. The Funding Opportunity Number for this announcement is **EPA-OEI-15-01**. Electronic applications must be submitted to this website by 11:59 pm on November 24, 2014. EPA advises applicants to submit their electronic applications early, so that if any technical difficulties arise, there will still be time to address them before the application deadline.

If you wish to apply electronically via grants.gov, the electronic submission of your application must be made by an official representative of your institution who is registered with grants.gov and authorized to sign applications for Federal assistance. For more information, on the registration requirements that must be completed in order to submit an application through grants.gov, go to http://www.grants.gov and click on "Applicants" on the top of the page then go to the "Get Registered" on the page. *Note that the registration process may take a week or longer.* If your organization is not currently registered with grants.gov, please encourage your office to designate an Authorized Organization Representative (AOR) and ask that individual to begin the registration process as soon as possible. Please note that the registration process also requires that your organization have a DUNS number and a current registration with the System for Award Management (SAM) and the process of obtaining both could take a month or more. Applicants must ensure that all registration requirements are met in order to apply for this opportunity through grants.gov and should ensure that all such requirements have been met well in advance of the submission deadline. Registration on grant.gov, SAM.gov, and DUNS number assignment is FREE.

To begin the application process under this grant announcement, go to http://www.grants.gov and click on "Apply for Grants" from the drop down menu and then follow the instructions accordingly. **Please Note: To apply through grants.gov you must use Adobe Reader software and download the compatible Adobe Reader version.** For more information about Adobe Reader, to verify compatibility, or to download the free software, please visit http://www.grants.gov/web/grants/support/technical-support/software/adobe-reader-compatibility.html

You may also be able to access the application package for this announcement by searching for the opportunity on http://www.grants.gov . Go to http://www.grants.gov and then click on "Search Grants" at the top of the page and enter the Funding Opportunity Number EPA-OEI-15-01, or the CFDA number that applies to this announcement (CFDA 66.608), in the appropriate field and click the Search button. Alternatively, you may be able to access the application package by clicking on the Application Package button at the top right of the synopsis page for the announcement on http://www.grants.gov . To find the synopsis page, go to http://www.grants.gov and click "Browse Agencies" in the middle of the page and then go to "Environmental Protection Agency" to find the EPA funding opportunities.

Please be sure to review the additional instructions below before applying electronically under this announcement through use of grants.gov that are available for download on grants.gov . You can also obtain additional instructions on completing and submitting the electronic application package by clicking the "Show Instructions" tab that is accessible within the application package itself.

Application materials submitted through grants.gov will be time/date stamped electronically. If you have not received a confirmation of receipt from EPA (not from grants.gov) within 30 days of the application deadline, please contact Salena Reynolds, Exchange Network Grant Program Manager, at (202)-566-0466 or reynolds.salena@epa.gov. Failure to do so may result in your application not being reviewed.

The forms and documents that comprise the applications will be either completed on-line in grants.gov or submitted as an attachment per **Figure E-1** below.

**Figure E-1**: Submission Instructions for Application Forms and Documents

| Form/Document | Submission Instruction |
|---|---|
| 1. Application for Federal Assistance (SF-424) | Complete on-line |
| 2. Budget Information for Non-Construction Programs (SF-424A) | Complete on-line |
| 3. Assurances for Non-Construction Programs (SF-424B) | Complete on-line |
| 4. Certification Regarding Lobbying Form | Complete on-line |
| 5. EPA Key Contacts Form 5700-54 | Complete on-line |
| 6. EPA Form 4700-4 – Preaward Compliance Review Report | Complete on-line |
| 7. Project Narrative | Attach document |
| 8. Detailed Itemized Budget (Budget Narrative Attachment Form) | Attach document |
| 9. Disclosure of Lobbying Activities (SF-LLL), if applicable | Complete on-line |
| 10. Negotiated Indirect Cost Rate Agreement, if applicable | Attach document |
| 11. Programmatic Resources and Personnel | Attach document |
| 12. Cover Letter | Attach document |
| 13. Additional Information for Inter-tribal Consortium, if applicable | Attach document |
| 14. Formal Project Partners Roles and Responsibilities, if applicable | Attach document |
| 15. List of Federally and/or Non-federally Funded Assistance | Attach document |

## Additional Application Preparation and Submission Instructions

**Documents 1 through 6** listed under Application Materials above should appear in the "Mandatory Documents" box on the Grants.gov Grant Application Package page. For documents 1 through 6, click on the appropriate form and then click "Open Form" below the box. The fields that must be completed will be highlighted in yellow. Optional fields and completed fields will be displayed in white. If you enter an invalid response or incomplete information in a field, you will receive an error message. When you have finished filling out each form, click "Save." When you return to the electronic Grant Application Package page, click on the form you just completed, and then click on the box that says, "Move Form to Submission List." This action will move the document over to the box that says, "Mandatory Completed Documents for Submission."

**Documents 7 and 8** require attached electronic files. Prepare your project narrative and detailed itemized budget as described above and save the documents to your computer as an MS Word or PDF file. When you are ready to attach your documents to the application package, click on "Project Narrative Attachment Form," and open the form. Click "Add Mandatory Project Narrative File," and then attach your documents (previously saved to your computer) using the browse window that appears. You may then click "View Mandatory Project Narrative File" to view it. Enter a brief descriptive title of your project in the space beside "Mandatory Project Narrative File Filename;" the filename should be no more than 40 characters long. If there are other attachments to submit to accompany your application, you may click "Add Optional Project Narrative File" and proceed as before. When you have finished attaching the necessary documents, click "Close Form." When you return to the "Grant Application Package" page, select the "Project Narrative Attachment Form" and click "Move Form to Submission List." The form should now appear in the box that says, "Mandatory Completed Documents for Submission." Follow the same general procedures for attaching document 8 – the Detailed Itemized Budget – using the "Budget Narrative Attachment Form."

**Documents 9 through 15** are listed in the "Optional Documents" box, but ***please note that these documents must be submitted as part of the application package, if applicable to your organization.*** To attach documents 9 through 16, use the "Other Attachments Form" in the "Optional Documents" box. After attaching the documents, please remember to highlight the "Other Attachments Form" and click "Move Form to Submission List" in order to move the documents to the box that says, "Optional Completed Documents for Submission.

Please note that applicants are limited to using the following characters in all attachment file names. Valid file names may only include the following UTF-8 characters: **A-Z, a-z, 0-9, underscore ( _ ), hyphen (-), space, period.** If applicants use any other characters when naming their attachment files their applications will be rejected by grants.gov.

Once you have finished filling out all of the forms/attachments and they appear in one of the "Completed Documents for Submission" boxes, click the "Save" button that appears at the top of the Web page. *It is suggested that you save the document a second time, using a different name, since this will make it easier to submit an amended package later, if necessary.* Please use the following format when saving your file: "Applicant Name – FY 2015 Exchange Network – 1st Submission" or "Applicant Name – FY 2015 Exchange Network – Back-up Submission." If it becomes necessary to submit an amended package at a later date, the name of the 2nd submission should be changed to "Applicant Name – FY 2015 Exchange Network – 2nd Submission."

Once your application package has been completed and saved, send it to your AOR for submission to U.S. EPA through grants.gov. Please advise your AOR to close all other software programs before attempting to submit the application package through grants.gov.

In the "Application Filing Name" box, your AOR should enter your organization's name and the words, "FY 2015 Exchange Network." The filing name should not exceed 40 characters (i.e., abbreviate where possible). From the "Grant Application Package" page, your AOR may submit the package by clicking the "Submit" button that appears at the top of the page. The AOR will then be asked to verify the agency and funding opportunity number for which the application package is submitted. If problems arise during the submission process, the AOR should reboot the computer before trying to submit the application package again. [It may be necessary to turn off the computer (not just restart it) or change computers before attempting to submit the package again.] If you continue to experience submission problems, the AOR may contact grants.gov for assistance at 1-800-518-4726 or email at http://www.grants.gov/help/help.jsp or call Salena Reynolds at 202-566-0466. You are encouraged to submit your application early, in case problems are encountered that result in delays.

## Suggested template for cover letter

*[Organizational Letterhead]*

Ms. Salena Reynolds
U.S. Environmental Protection Agency
Office of Environmental Information
1200 Pennsylvania Ave., NW, Mail Code 2823-T
Washington, DC 20460

Dear Ms. Reynolds:

I am pleased to submit the [state, tribe or territory name here] [Name of Department or Agency]'s application for a [**type of assistance**: grant, cooperative agreement], entitled [project name], under the FY 2015 Exchange Network Grant Program. This application is for an [**Exchange Network or E-Enterprise-related**] category of EN project. This application is seeking [dollar amount] in direct grants funding and [dollar amount of Funds] in in-kind support. We have ['no' or number of partners] formal partners in this grant application. [Our partners are: name partners].

[Short narrative description of project including a statement of project goal(s)]

The contact for this grant application is:

Name and Title of Project Lead
Name of Office or Division
Name of Department or Agency
Full Mailing Address
Phone
Number(s)
Email address

If there are any questions, please feel free to call either myself or the contact named in this letter.

Sincerely,
**[Name/Title of Authorized Organizational Representative]**

Attachment

# Appendix E

## Sample Project Goals, Outputs, and Outcomes

### Goals

**1. Emissions Inventory System (EIS) & Greenhouse Gas (GHG) Dataflows**
Freedonia DEP has been sending NEI data to EPA using the Exchange Network. However, as EPA moves to a new database, called the Emissions Inventory System, this dataflow will need to be upgraded to meet the new schema, CERS.

Freedonia requires Title V facilities to provide Greenhouse Gas (GHG) data to the state, unless they are providing data directly to The Climate Registry (TCR). Currently three Freedonia companies have agreed to supply data to TCR. The remainder of the Title V facilities must supply GHG data to Freedonia DEP annually using the same online system as NEI data. This system is called the **Permitting and Air Reporting System of Freedonia (PARSOF)**.

1.1. **Map EIS & GHG data elements** to the CERS XML Schema.
This includes detailed analysis and specifications for transferring data from PARSOF to CERS schema.

1.2. Implement the **production EIS dataflow**. This includes:
- Develop the Extract, Transform and Load (ETL) process to load PARSOF data to staging tables
- Develop an EIS node plug-in to transfer the data from the staging tables to XML
- Configure the node dataflow
- Test the dataflow and perform quality assessment

1.3. Implement the **GHG dataflow** to production.
Repeat step 1.2 with minor adaptations for GHG data.

1.4. Improve **GIS Locations** for emission points from Title V facilities, including preparation of geospatial metadata for the Latitude/Longitude Data Standard and meeting EPA's minimum accuracy of 25 meters for most points. This will improve the accuracy of data in both EIS and GHG.

This includes obtaining and entering locations and stack parameters for approximately 9,500 emission points into the PARSOF database. Some of these data will need to be transformed from the Breeze modeling software, and some obtained from paper maps and checked against aerial photos. Also if time allows, other locations and associated Web applications for environmental assessment/integration may be improved.

1.5. Add **application module** to the Facility Explorer Web application **to allow easy access to emission point locations** and associated data. This will be used to evaluate emission rates of surrounding major facilities within a given radius of a proposed construction project.

This is a required assessment under the Prevention of Significant Deterioration (PSD) permitting program.

Currently when a construction project is proposed, the applicant contacts DEP who then queries the database for nearby sites, and manually finds the emission point data for each site to send to the applicant. The proposed Web application module will allow the applicant to run a simple query themselves, thus obtaining the data immediately, and completely eliminating the need for DEP staff to find data.

The proposed application module includes programming to load the emission point locations as sub-entities into Freedonia's Environmental Facilities Database (EFD) warehouse, request the search, do the GIS query, retrieve needed report data from EFD and PARSOF, and build the report using SQL Reporting Services. The report will include:
- **facility** name, address, and plant ID;
- permitted or potential facility-wide **emission rates** in tons per year for: $SO_2$, NOx, CO, Pb, $PM_{10}$, and (if available) $PM_{2.5}$;
- a list of **emission point locations** with XY coordinates in UTM;
- permitted or potential **emission rates** and the most recent two years of actual emissions for each emission point for: $SO_2$, NOx, CO, Pb, $PM_{10}$, and (if available) $PM_{2.5}$; and
- **stack parameters**, including stack ID, height, diameter, temperature, flow rate, emission point type, bypass stack (Y/N), and obstructed (Y/N).

## 2. Water Quality Exchange (WQX) Flow

The replacement database for STORET, AWQMS (Ambient Water Quality Management System) is being developed by several states and Region 8, including Illinois, Minnesota, Utah, the National Park Service, and possibly Alaska. Freedonia is planning to implement this database to replace Freedonia STORET as the state database.

2.1. **Map** the data elements to the XML Schema. This includes detailed analysis and specifications for transferring data from the state database to WQX schema.

2.2. **Implement** the dataflow to CDX (EPA's Node). This includes:
- adapt the 4.1 WQX Windsor node plug-in to transfer the data from the state database to XML;
- set up and configure the node; and
- test the dataflow and perform quality assessment.

2.3. **Document the flow implementation** for use by other states using AWQMS and the same type of Node. Illinois and Minnesota use a Windsor .NET node. Other agencies have also mentioned the possibility of using the Windsor Node by the time this is implemented. Freedonia DEP will develop the documentation and provide any applicable code to these other agencies for streamlined implementation.

2.4. Publish a **Web service** that will allow applications to pull water quality monitoring data. This Web service will allow applications to query water quality monitoring data from the state's database. Initial plans are for at least two staging tables which can be populated using an automated DTS/SSIS or other script.

At a minimum, the staging tables should include the following elements and any other required elements in the WQX schema.

The output will be in WQX standard XML and include all elements in the staging tables. This grant will focus on making this work with Freedonia data. However, this can be extended later in two ways:
- add data to Freedonia's staging tables from other sources, such as USGS, the Freedonia Pesticide Monitoring database (FPEST), and raw water samples from the Safe Drinking Water Information System (SDWIS). This will allow applications to pull easily pull monitoring data from a variety of sources; or
- share the code and documentation with other states using AWQMS.

### Figure F-1: Goals, Outputs, Target Dates, and Outcomes

| Goal | Output | Target Date[1] | Outcome |
|---|---|---|---|
| EIS & GHG Dataflows | 1.1 CERS data mapped to XML schema | Jan. 1, 2016 | Increased availability of timely, high quality data to other Exchange Network partners will improve environmental decision-making. |
| | 1.2 EIS flow to EPA becomes operational | June 1, 2016 | |
| | 1.3 GHG flow to EPA becomes operational[2] | Dec. 31, 2016 | |
| | 1.4 Improve GIS locations & geospatial metadata for air release | Sept. 30, 2017 | |
| | 1.5 Add Assessment Module[3] to evaluate air | Mar. 31, 2018 | |
| WQX[4] | 2.1 Data mapped to XML schema[2] | Mar. 31, 2016 | Increased availability of data to other Exchange Network partners Electronic availability of standardized, timely, high quality data over the Exchange Network will improve the analysis of water quality monitoring data and lead to better |
| | 2.2 Implement WQX | Sept. 30, 2016 | |
| | 2.3 Written documentation of implementing WQX with | Jan. 31, 2017 | |
| | 2.4 Publish Web service | Sept. 30, 2017 | |

[1] Estimated Grant Period: October 1, 2015 through Sept. 30, 2018. If DEP is notified of the grant award by August 1 or before, dates will be shifted so they fall within the grant period.
[2] These tasks also accomplish the following intermediate outcome:
- **Improved business processes** that facilitate **burden reduction** on the regulated community.
[3] These tasks also accomplish the following two intermediate outcomes:

- **Increased speed and timeliness of data exchange** by allowing data exchanges to happen more frequently, thereby decreasing the lag between partner systems;
- – • **Increased efficiency** of data exchange by reducing administrative burden, including reducing or eliminating manual intervention for tasks such as scheduling, resubmissions, or security.

[4]This goal also accomplishes the following intermediate outcomes.

- Economies of scale through shared infrastructure to achieve **reduced costs and expanded functionality**.

Please see our attached Detailed Budget which links expected investments under this agreement to each goal to support and complete the proposed work referenced in this Narrative.

# Appendix F

## Contracts and Subawards

**Can funding be used for the applicant to make subawards, acquire contract services or fund partnerships?**

EPA awards funds to one eligible applicant as the recipient even if other eligible applicants are named as partners or co-applicants or members of a coalition or consortium. The recipient is accountable to EPA for the proper expenditure of funds.

Funding may be used to provide subgrants or subawards of financial assistance, which includes using subawards or subgrants to fund partnerships, provided the recipient complies with applicable requirements for subawards or subgrants including those contained in 40 CFR Parts 30 or 31, as appropriate. Applicants must compete contracts for services and products, including consultant contracts, and conduct cost and price analyses to the extent required by the procurement provisions of the regulations at 40 CFR Parts 30 or 31, as appropriate. The regulations also contain limitations on consultant compensation. Applicants are not required to identify subawardees/subgrantees and/or contractors (including consultants) in their application. However, if they do, the fact that an applicant selected for award has named a specific subawardee/subgrantee, contractor, or consultant in the application EPA selects for funding does not relieve the applicant of its obligations to comply with subaward/subgrant and/or competitive procurement requirements as appropriate. Please note that applicants may not award sole source contracts to consulting, engineering or other firms assisting applicants with the application solely based on the firm's role in preparing the application.

Successful applicants cannot use subgrants or subawards to avoid requirements in EPA grant regulations for competitive procurement by using these instruments to acquire commercial services or products from for-profit organizations to carry out its assistance agreement. The nature of the transaction between the recipient and the subawardee or subgrantee must be consistent with the standards for distinguishing between vendor transactions and subrecipient assistance under Subpart B Section .210 of OMB Circular A-133 , and the definitions of subaward at 40 CFR 30.2(ff) or subgrant at 40 CFR 31.3, as applicable. EPA will not be a party to these transactions. Applicants acquiring commercial goods or services must comply with the competitive procurement standards in 40 CFR Part 30 or 40 CFR Part 31.36 and cannot use a subaward/subgrant as the funding mechanism.

**How will an applicant's proposed subawardees/subgrantees and contractors be considered during the evaluation process described in Section V of the announcement?**

Section V of the announcement describes the evaluation criteria and evaluation process that will be used by EPA to make selections under this announcement. During this evaluation, except for those criteria that relate to the applicant's own qualifications, past performance, and reporting history, the review panel will consider, if appropriate and relevant, the qualifications, expertise, and experience of:

(i) an applicant's named subawardees/subgrantees identified in the application if the applicant demonstrates in the application that if it receives an award that the subaward/subgrant will be properly awarded consistent with the applicable regulations in 40 CFR Parts 30 or 31. For example, applicants must not use subawards/subgrants to obtain commercial services or products from for profit firms or individual consultants.
(ii) an applicant's named contractor(s), including consultants, identified in the application if the applicant demonstrates in its application that the contractor(s) was selected in compliance with the competitive Procurement Standards in 40 CFR Part 30 or 40 CFR 31.36 as appropriate. For example, an applicant must demonstrate that it selected the contractor(s) competitively or that a proper non-competitive sole-source award consistent with the regulations will be made to the contractor(s), that efforts were made to provide small and disadvantaged businesses with opportunities to compete, and that some form of cost or price analysis was conducted. EPA may not accept sole source justifications for contracts for services or products that are otherwise readily available in the commercial marketplace.

EPA will not consider the qualifications, experience, and expertise of named subawardees/subgrantees and/or named contractor(s) during the application evaluation process unless the applicant complies with these requirements.

**How can I report information subawards?**
To report subaward information is FSRS, you must have an account. To register in FSRS, follow the instructions below:

Step 1: Access the FSRS online home page (https://www.fsrs.gov/)
Step 2: Click on "Awardees" in the "log-in or register now" box on the home page.
Step 3: Click on "Registration Instructions for Awardees" under the returning awardees; login fields.

FSRS also developed an awardee user guide with step by step instructions on submitting a report, https://www.fsrs.gov/documents/FSRS_Awardee_User_Guide.pdf

# Appendix G

## Checklist of Documents to Submit

The following documents are required under this Solicitation Notice and constitute the full application to EPA for assistance agreement funding. Fillable forms can be obtained from (http://www.epa.gov/ogd/forms/forms.htm). All applicable forms and documents must be submitted and validated within grants.gov, postmarked, or delivered by an overnight courier service **at or before 11:59pm on  November 24, 2014**. To confirm applicant eligibility and/or applicability of any of the listed forms or documents below, please contact Salena Reynolds at (202) 566-0466 or reynolds.salena@epa.gov.

- ☐ Standard Form 424, "Applications for Federal Assistance"
- ☐ Standard Form 424A, "Budget Information for Non Construction Programs"
- ☐ Standard Form 424B, "Assurances for Non Construction Programs"
- ☐ Certification Regarding Lobbying Form
- ☐ Standard Form 5700-54, "Key Contacts Form"
- ☐ EPA Form 4700-4, "Preaward Compliance Review Report"
- ☐ Project Narrative
  - o No more than 10-pages, single-spaced.
  - o Must address Evaluation Criteria [Section V-A] and link activities to results/outcomes.
- ☐ Detailed Itemized Budget
  - o Describe both total project budget and the costs associated with each major goal.
  - o If budget includes indirect costs, an approved IDC Agreement is required.
- ☐ Standard Form LLL, "Disclosure of Lobbying Activities", if applicable
- ☐ Negotiated Indirect Cost Agreement, if applicable
- ☐ Programmatic Resources and Personnel
- ☐ Cover Letter
  - o  Recipient Information
  - o Indicate if application is for traditional Phase 2 (or Phase 1) Exchange Network priorities or E-Enterprise related category
  - o  Project Title
  - o  Type of Assistance Vehicle identified *[Section II-B]*
  - o  Partners, if applicable *[Section III-C]*
  - o  Brief Project Summary
  - o  Contact Information for Project Lead
  - o  Signature of Executive as Authorized Organizational Representative
- ☐ Description of Inter-Tribal Consortium Eligibility, if applicable
- ☐ Formal Project Partners, if applicable
  - o  Project Narrative *[above]* details roles and responsibilities of lead and partners in carrying out each project goal.
  - o  If lead will distribute funding to partners, describe methodology or state no distribution.
  - o  Letters of support and intent included from all proposed partners.
- ☐  List of EN Assistance Agreements

# Appendix H — Quality Assurance Reporting Form

OMB No. 2025-0006
Expires 4/30/2015

## U.S. ENVIRONMENTAL PROTECTION AGENCY
### Quality Assurance Reporting Form
### for Use by Recipients of Assistance Agreements

**Recipient Organization:**

EPA Award Number:

Name:

Address:

Project/Program Period (starting and ending dates, mm/dd/yyyy):

**Activity Group:**
(check all that apply)

☐ Infrastructure Development
☐ Data Exchange, Analysis and Integration
☐ Planning, Mentoring, and Training
☐ Challenge

| Goal | Task | Output | Outcome | Quality Assurance Measures |
|------|------|--------|---------|-----------------------------|
|      |      |        |         |                             |
|      |      |        |         |                             |

**Instructions:**
- Please submit electronically to your project officer within 90 days of award.
- For Quality Assurance Measures, please refer to current Solicitation Notice for Quality Assurance Guidelines.
- For Goals, please refer to goals outlined in your assistance agreement work plan.

**Paperwork Reduction Act (PRA) Burden Statement:** The public reporting and recordkeeping burden for this collection of information is estimated to average one hour per response. Send comments on the Agency's need for this information, the accuracy of the provided burden estimates, and any suggested methods for minimizing respondent burden, including through the use of automated collection techniques to the Director, Collection Strategies Division, U.S. Environmental Protection Agency (2822T), 1200 Pennsylvania Ave., NW, Washington, D.C. 20460. Include the OMB control number in any correspondence. Do not send the completed form to this address.

# Appendix I

## Reusability: RCS and ENDS

### What is Reusability?
Reusability, as related to the Exchange Network and the grants, has a broad definition. It could mean exact reuse, such as employing a widget or mobile application as developed and available, or simply discovering similar tools that are out there and perhaps seeking best practices therein. It is difficult to deem an asset reusable or not because reusability is only limited by the willingness and creativity of its developers and users.

Some examples of reusability include:
- using components of an existing CROMERR compliant tool to develop your own tool that is CROMERR compliant;
- modifying existing java code to perform a similar function;
- learning best practices in the development of your new REST Web service from someone who has developed similar Web services;
- pooling resources to develop a software tool that will benefit multiple states;
- using existing Web services to authenticate access to CDX instead of developing your own; and
- new or updated map templates, geospatial data Web services or geoprocessing tools that address commonly occurring challenges.

### Benefits of Reusability
- Cost: adapting and integrating costs less than building. Saves taxpayer dollars.
- Speed: faster than building from scratch. Reusable assets have been implemented before and comply with requirements and security restraints.
- Quality: reuse leads to the discovery and correction of defects and overall product improvement.
- Environmental: reusing tools and building tools for future reuse saves resources.

### Tips for Creating Reusable Tools
The extent to which a resource is considered reusable varies widely. However, when developing a new resource, there are certain principles one can follow to make the resource more available for reuse:
- the resource and its architecture have comprehensive documentation;
- the resource is 'portable' in that it does not rely heavily on a specific hardware or technology;
- the resource is flexible and can perform multiple functions;
- the resource is compliant with existing standards; and
- the resource is reliable and free of defects.

*Please visit www.epa.gov/rcs to begin searching for reusable resources.*

## How to Register in RCS:

### Searching RCS for reusable resources

Anyone can search RCS by going to www.epa.gov/rcs. All resources designated as publicly-viewable can be found here. To see resources marked as only available to EPA and partners, you must login to RCS. Please see below for instructions on accessing the non-public version of RCS.

### Requesting Access to the non-public version of RCS

1. Go to www.epa.gov/sor

2. On the left side menu, select "Login for EPA & Partners"

3. If you have an EPA LAN ID and password, you may enter it now. If not, select the link below the login box that says "CLICK HERE to register for access to the EPA Portal."

4. Enter the requested information on the next screen

5. Click "continue." Another fillable screen displays. For EPA sponsor, enter Lico Galindo, galindo.lico@epa.gov. For Community of Interest, select "System of Registries." For Reason for Access, select "RCS access"

6. Click "submit." You will receive an approval email in 1-2 days

### Registering an IT Resource in RCS

1. Log in to RCS. Go to the Asset Catalog in either Browse or Search mode

2. Click "Add Asset" (near the middle of the page)

3. Fill out the requested information:

a. Name (i.e. Iowa RiverMapper)
b. Description (i.e. A software tool that allows users to map river data around the state of Iowa)
c. Version (this will likely be Version 1)
d. Organization (choose "U.S. EPA and Partners")

4. Click "OK." The full record of the new resource will display.

5. Fill out the appropriate information in the tabs, such as information about the steward of this asset. Please note that not all tabs need to be filled in; rather, any important metadata or information relevant to the resource should be provided. Every resource should have a steward.

6. The new resource will be reviewed by the RCS Registrar. Until approved by him, it will only be visible to you.

**What should be registered in RCS?**

Block of Code- pieces of programming code that perform a specific function that can be used in whole or in part, as-is or modified, in developing software.

Software Tool- any piece of software (utility, application, etc.) that performs one or more functions.

System- software that performs one or more specific tasks. *Example: the Integrated Compliance Information System, or ICIS*

Widget- a software tool that uses a small graphical interface to provide a function or service to a Web application or Web page. *Example: the UV Index widget*

Web Service- software system designed to support machine-to-machine interaction over a network. These can be either SOAP (Simple Object Access Protocol) or REST (Representational State Transfer). *Examples: the FRS Facility Search REST Web service; the Convert Lat/Long SOAP Web service*

XML Schema- XML language description of the structure and content of a document or data set.

Mobile App- a software tool that runs on a portable device such as a Smartphone or tablet.

*\*The types of IT resources listed above are some of the most common and important types to add to RCS. However, there are other types of resources that can be registered. Please check in RCS to see a full list.*

***\*\*\*Please do not hesitate to contact Lico Galindo (galindo.lico@epa.gov, 202-566-1252) if you have any questions at all regarding problems accessing RCS, what or how to register, or if you would like some hands-on help or a demo of RCS.***

**Searching for reusable dataflows and services in ENDS**

The recipient shall reuse existing dataflow names and Exchange Network services registered in ENDS, instead of building new ones, for sharing similar data over the Exchange Network. To research what resources exist, the recipient shall review what is registered at http://www.exchangenetwork.net and have an Exchange Network node administrator check in the production ENDS Web site located at https://ends2.epa.gov/admin/default.aspx. ENDS supports copying existing service definitions in order to simplify this reuse.

**Registering new Exchange Network resources to ENDS:**

The recipient shall enter metadata and descriptions of all new Exchange Network nodes, dataflows and services developed under this grant into the Exchange Network Discovery Services v2.0. Registering information in ENDS is described at http://www.exchangenetwork.net/exchange-network-discovery-service-ends and in detail in the Discovery Users Guide V3 at http://www.exchangenetwork.net/node/DiscoveryUserGuidev3.doc. In order to register new resources in ENDS, the recipient will need a NAAS account with node administrator access rights. Such account needs to be requested at the Exchange Network help desk at 888-890-1995 nodehelpdesk@epacdx.net.

**What should be registered in ENDS?**

<u>Exchange Network nodes used to deploy services.</u>

<u>Dataflows – Processes used in the exchange</u> of information between two or more network partners.

Exchange Network Services – Web services that implement dataflows are special services that need a Flow Control Document and other special documents to describe the service. Please refer to the Discovery Users Guide V3 at http://www.exchangenetwork.net/node/DiscoveryUserGuidev3.doc.

***<u>*Please*</u> contact the Exchange Network help desk (nodehelpdesk@epacdx.net , 888-890-1995) if you have any questions at all regarding problems accessing ENDS, what or how to register.*

The following table shows where the different resources should be registered:

| Service or Component Type | Register in ENDS | Register in RCS |
|---|---|---|
| Network nodes | X | |
| Dataflows | X | |
| EN services (related to dataflows) | X | |
| XML Schema | | X |
| Software Tools | | X |
| Web services not related to dataflows, SOAP or REST | | X |
| Widget tools | | X |
| Programming Code (routines, classes, etc.) | | X |
| Mobile Applications | | X |
| Code Libraries | | X |

| Others | PLEASE DISCUSS WITH YOUR REGIONAL COORDINATOR |
|---|---|

## Definitions

### Application Programming Interface (API)

When used in the context of web development, an API is typically defined as a set of Hypertext Transfer Protocol (HTTP) request messages, along with a definition of the structure of response messages, which is usually in an Extensible Markup Language (XML) or JavaScript Object Notation (JSON) format. The term web API is virtually synonymous with the term web service.

### Central Data Exchange (CDX)

EPA's CDX is the point of entry to the National Environmental Information Exchange Network (Exchange Network) for environmental data exchanges to the Agency. CDX provides the capability for submitters to access their data through the use of Web services. CDX enables EPA and participating Program Offices to work with stakeholders - including state, tribal and local governments and regulated industries - to enable streamlined, electronic submission of data via the Internet.

### Community of Interest

A community of interest is a group of Exchange Network stakeholders who share an interest in the exchange of a specific set of environmental data.

### Construction

Construction is the erection, building, alteration, remodeling, improvement, or extension of buildings, structures or other property. Construction also includes remedial actions in response to a release, or a threat of a release, of a hazardous substance into the environment as determined by the Comprehensive Environmental Response, Compensation, and Liability Act (CERCLA) of 1980.

### Cross-Media Electronic Reporting Regulation (CROMERR)

Regulation that sets requirements – including performance-based, technology-neutral standards for electronic reporting systems – for states, tribes and local governments implementing electronic reporting under their approved EPA-authorized programs. CROMERR requires that states, tribes, and local governments amend or revise their EPA-authorized program(s) to receive reports from regulated facilities under those programs. Both new and existing electronic reporting programs require EPA approval, and the regulation establishes a process for applying for and obtaining such approval. CROMERR also addresses electronic reporting directly to EPA.

### Data Access Services (Publishing)

Network publishing is a term that refers to using Exchange Network technologies, services and specifications for Web services to make data available to Network users by querying nodes and returning environmental data in the form of XML or (Json) documents. These services are also called data services. Once these data services are deployed, they can be used in a number of ways such as populating Web pages, synchronizing data between sites, viewing data in a Web service client, or building new sources of data into an integrated application. In other words, data access services are a specific subset of the many possible types of Web services. Other Web service types include data submission, security, quality assurance, notification and status.

## Data Element

A data element is the smallest unit of information stored in and exchanged among Exchange Network partners' information systems. Examples of data elements are the facility name, DUNS number, and inspection date.

## Data Exchange Template (DET)

A data exchange template is a standardized format that identifies the types of information required/allowed in a particular document or data exchange. Data exchange templates contain no data, but they define the format for exchange according to data standards and trading partner agreements. A standard template for DET's is available on the Exchange Network website (http://www.exchangenetwork.net/knowledge-base/).

## Data Standard

A data standard documents an agreement on representation, format, and definition of common data exchanged. Exchange Network partners must use data standards that have been approved by the Exchange Network Leadership Council (ENLC). The ENLC has subsumed the activities of the Environmental Data Standards Council (EDSC). See information at http://www.exchangenetwork.net/knowledge-base/

## E-Enterprise

E-Enterprise is a joint initiative of States and EPA to expand access to environmental monitoring data, streamline regulatory information collections, and achieve performance goals for regulatory burden reduction and cost avoidance. The E-Enterprise program will be institutionalized through policies, supported by shared services, coordinated with governmental partners, and overseen by intra-agency and interagency governance structures.

## Enhancement

An enhancement is defined as expanding geographic coverage, or adding new data elements, additional parameters, or historical data to an existing national or priority data exchange or schema.

## Exchange Network Discovery Services (ENDS)

The Exchange Network Discovery Services (ENDS) is a set of directory services for all nodes in Exchange Network. This central catalog approach supports the automated consumption of services using tools such as the EN Browser and the EN Services Center via an XML document that contains the service metadata. ENDS automates both the discovery and retrieval of service metadata for the Network and supports the Administration and export of node services via the Web and Web Service interfaces. ENDS is composed of two main components: the first, is a set of services that allows EN partners to submit and query the service descriptions stored in the ENDS repository; the second, is a Web interface that simplifies the data entry of service metadata into ENDS. The services all accept or return a common XML schema. This XML schema provides a structured, standard way to represent EN services across all EN Nodes. A second ENDS schema defines the Data Element Description Language (DEDL) that can be used by individual Exchange Network nodes for describing acceptable parameters and valid allowable values, and making them available as services. DEDL further enhances the ability for EN partners to build rich, user friendly applications using EN services. More information on ENDS is available at http://www.exchangenetwork.net/exchange-network-discovery-service-ends/.

## Exchange Network Services Center (ENSC)

The ENSC is a browser based portal that provides Exchange Network partners access to a broad range of Network services. Among the most notable features of the Service Center is the ability to submit data to EPA systems, monitor the status of data submissions, and access a variety of Network administrative data. Essentially, the ENSC offers most of the functionality of a Node, but it is not automated and cannot respond to data requests. It simplifies access to Network services because it requires no software to install or configure. It can be accessed from any computer with a browser and internet access. The ENSC is available at https://enservices.epa.gov/login.aspx.

## Environmental Information Exchange Network (Exchange Network)

The Exchange Network is an Internet and standards-based information network among EPA and its partners in states, tribes, and territories. It is designed to help integrate information, provide secure real-time access to environmental information, and support the electronic collection and exchange of high-quality data and information. The Exchange Network provides a more efficient way of exchanging environmental information at all levels of government. It significantly improves the way EPA and its state, tribal, and territorial partners send and receive information.

## Extensible Markup Language (XML)

Extensible Markup Language is a flexible language for creating common information formats and sharing both the format and content of data over the Internet and elsewhere. XML is a formatting language recommended by the World Wide Web Consortium (W3C). For guidance on the development of XML schema for the Exchange Network or related activities of the Network Technical Group, see the Exchange Network website at http://www.exchangenetwork.net.

## Flow Configuration Documents (FCDs)

FCDs are the principle document that captures the detailed data exchange processing design and roles governing the data exchange using narrative text, diagrams and examples. A standard template for FCDs is available on the Exchange Network website at http://www.exchangenetwork.net/knowledge-base/.

## Geographic Information Systems

Geographic Information Systems (GIS) include software and hardware systems that relate and display collected data in terms of geographic or spatial location. GIS allow users to collect, manage, and analyze large volumes of geospatial data and metadata. EPA and its partners use GIS systems to conduct complex environmental analyses.

## Geospatial Data

Geospatial data are data that identify, depict, or describe the geographic locations, boundaries, or characteristics of the Earth's inhabitants or its natural or human-constructed features. Geospatial data include geographic coordinates (e.g., latitude and longitude) that identify a specific location on the Earth and data that are linked to geographic locations or have a geospatial component (e.g., socio-economic data, land use records and analyses, land surveys, homeland security information, and environmental analyses). Geospatial data may be obtained using a variety of approaches and technologies, including things such as surveys, satellite remote sensing, Global Position System (GPS) hand-held devices, and airborne imagery and detection devices.

## Geospatial Technologies

Geospatial technologies include the computer hardware and software that are commonly used to collect, import, store, manipulate, analyze, and display digital geospatial data. These technologies include GIS, global positioning systems (GPS), remote sensing and visualization systems.

## In-Kind Services

Services provided by EPA contractors and consultants on specific parts of the project for the recipient. The recipient can request this type of service as part of the grant application, if the in- kind work is directly related to the recipient's application and the applicant is the primary beneficiary of the work. However, EPA reserves the right to decide whether or not in-kind services will be provided. The recipient may not direct the work provided through in-kind services. These services are managed by EPA.

## Integrated Project Team

A group of individuals comprised of partner and EPA staff, support contractors, and technology vendors organized to design and implement a specific exchange.

## Metadata

Metadata are data or information that describes other data. Examples include data that describe how or where the data were collected, whether or not the data comply with agreed-upon data standards, or how the data will be used.

## Network Authorization and Authentication Services (NAAS)

Network Authorization and Authentication Services (NAAS) are a set of centralized information security services that Exchange Network partners can use to authenticate and authorize their users. NAAS provides an efficient way for Exchange Network participants to exchange data, without having to build and maintain their own security system. NAAS supports many levels of security, from PIN/passwords to public Key Infrastructure. All NAAS operations are conducted over a Secure Socket Layer (SSL) channel using 128-bit encryption.

## Node

A Node is a Web service enabled server (hardware and software) that provides a point for exchanging information over the Internet. Exchange Network Nodes can gain access to and transmit information using Web services. In order to achieve interoperability among Nodes, all Nodes must be set up according to the Exchange Network specifications. Freely available Node software is available at http://www.exchangenetwork.net/exchange-network-products/. Specifications, protocols, tools, code and documentation for building a functioning Exchange Network Node are available at http://www.exchangenetwork.net/knowledge-base/ .

## Node Client

A Node client is an application (software code) that can generate Web service messages for using the Exchange Network. A Node client can do the following:

- Submit data in XML format to EPA or other partners using the Exchange Network and
- Request data in XML format from EPA or other partners using the Exchange Network.

Several Node clients that are very user friendly are available on the Exchange Network website already. More are on the way. A Node client software developer kit (SDK) is also available to help you integrate Node client requests into your applications. Unlike Nodes, Node clients *cannot* publish data on the Exchange Network (i.e., they cannot listen for or respond to data queries from other Exchange Network partners)

## Outcome

The term "outcome" means the result, effect, or consequence of carrying out a project leading to an environmental or programmatic goal. Outcomes may be environmental, behavioral, health- related or programmatic in nature, may be quantitative or qualitative, and may not necessarily be achievable within an assistance agreement funding period.

## Output

The term "output" means an environmental activity, effort, or associated work products leading to an environmental goal, that will be produced or provided over a period of time or by a specified date. Outputs may be quantitative or qualitative but must be measurable during an assistance agreement funding period.

## Phase 1 (of the Exchange Network)
Phase 1 of the Exchange Network is a term that the Network community uses to identify the Ten National and Priority System Flows identified in this Solicitation Notice. The flows are: Air Quality System (AQS); Emissions Inventory System (EIS); Integrated Compliance Information System – National Pollution Discharge Elimination System (ICIS-NPDES), including Net Discharge Monitoring Reports (NetDMR); Resource Conservation and Recovery Act Information System (RCRAinfo); eBeaches; Safe Drinking Water Information System (SDWIS); Underground Injection Control Database (UIC); Water Quality Exchange (WQX); Facility Registry System (FRS); and Toxic Release Inventory System (TRIS).

## Phase 2 (of the Exchange Network)
Phase 2 of the Exchange Network is the term that the Network community uses to refer to the second phase of Network development. Phase 1 focused on development of the Network infrastructure and implementation of data reporting to EPA using the Network. In Phase 2, the Network community will expand Network publishing (data owners making their information available to other partners on the Network using automated services), develop applications (both mobile and desktop) and websites (including public sites) that analyze and/or display data accessed using Exchange Network services, expand the use of the Network for data reporting to additional EPA data systems, expand intra-partner data sharing including programs where EPA does not have a central data store (e.g. institutional controls for cleanup sites) and develop new technologies that make using the Network easier and less costly.

## Representational State Transfer (REST) / RESTful Web Service
Software system designed to support machine-to-machine interaction over a network. Representational State Transfer (REST) services do not require XML, SOAP, or WSDL (Web Services Description Language) but rely on the exchange of requests and responses between the resources and on their corresponding states. REST-style services facilitate the aggregation of services into more complex services and the development of mashups. REST services are usually accessed via HTTP (like a Web URL or link). Guidance on implementing REST services for the Exchange Network is available at http://www.exchangenetwork.net/rest-guidance/.

## Reusable Component Services (RCS)
Reusable Component Services (RCS) is a catalog of information technology resources (e.g., XML schema, widgets, REST Web services) from U.S. EPA, states tribes and other partners that provides a central point of access to a broad range of components and services. RCS promotes effective information management by centrally registering these resources, and it enables reuse of those resources for the purposes of reducing cost, speeding development, and producing higher-quality systems. RCS is located at http://www.epa.gov/rcs.

## Schema

An XML schema defines the structure of an XML document including data elements and attributes can appear in a document; how the data elements relate to one another; whether an element is empty or can include text; which types of data are allowed for specific data elements and attributes; and what the default and fixed values are for elements and attributes. A set of Network quality assurance Web services is available to validate your XML documents against the schemas using a standard parser. A list of procedural and guidance documents related to schema development is available on the Exchange Network website at http://www.exchangenetwork.net/knowledge-base/ .

## Schematron

Schematron is an open source application that is used for validating XML documents against business rules and returning error reports. It uses XML stylesheet (XSLT) technology. The Network Quality Assurance Services use Schematron to validate XML documents against the business rules, as well as supporting a standard parser for schema validation.

## Simple Object Access Protocol (SOAP)

SOAP is a protocol specification for exchanging structured information for the implementation of Web services on a computer network. It allows machines to interoperate in a loosely coupled manner using simple standard messages over the Hypertext Transfer Protocol (HTTP or others) and uses Extensible Markup Language (XML) as the mechanisms for information exchange.

## Virtual Node

A Virtual Node is a central node server that can host any number of partner nodes: state, tribe, region, agency, etc. Each partner node is simply configured using wizards and forms on the central virtual node cloud server. This eliminates the need for maintaining a local node completely. Each partner node functions like a conventional node, only it is much simpler and less expensive to set up and maintain.

## Web Form

A standard interface that can be downloaded from the Internet, a Web form contains blank fields for a user to enter data and submit the form (e.g., environmental reports) to the receiver.

## Web Services

Web services are a software system designed to support interoperable machine-to-machine interaction over a network. They make it easier to conduct work across organizations regardless of the types of operating systems, hardware/software, programming languages, and databases that are being used.

## Widget

A software tool that uses a small (smaller than a page) graphical interface to provide a function or service and that can be added to a Web application or to a Web page.